A Discourse of the House of the Forest of Lebanon

By: John Bunyan

John Bunyan

1628-1688

INTRODUCTION

John Bunyan (28 November 1628 – 31 August 1688) was an English Christian writer and preacher, famous for writing The Pilgrim's Progress. Though he was a Reformed Baptist, in the Church of England he is remembered with a Lesser Festival on 30 August, and on the liturgical calendar of the Episcopal Church (USA) on August 29. As his popularity and notoriety grew, Bunyan increasingly became a target for slander and libel; he was described as "a witch, a Jesuit, a highwayman" and was said to have mistresses and multiple wives.

In 1658, aged 30, he was arrested for preaching at Eaton Socon and indicted for preaching without a licence. He continued preaching, however, and did not suffer imprisonment until November 1660, when he was taken to the County gaol in Silver Street, Bedford. In that same year, Bunyan married his second wife, Elizabeth, by whom he had two more children, Sarah and Joseph. The Restoration of the monarchy by Charles II of England began Bunyan's persecution as England returned to Anglicanism. Meeting-houses were quickly closed and all citizens were required to attend their Anglican parish church. It became punishable by law to "conduct divine service except in accordance with the ritual of the church, or for one not in Episcopal orders to address a congregation." Thus, John Bunyan no longer had that freedom to preach which he had enjoyed under the Puritan Commonwealth. He was arrested on 12 November 1660, whilst preaching privately in Lower Samsell by Harlington, Bedfordshire, 10 miles south of Bedford.

Bunyan in prison

Bunyan's home

Bunyan in prison

Bunyan preaching

Bust of Bunyan

A
Discourse
O F,
The House of the Forest of Lebanon.
This House distinct from the Temple at Jerusalem, which
was a type of the Church in her worshipping state, as the House
at Lebanon is a type of the Church in the wilderness, or in
sackcloth; larger than the Temple; all its parts spiritualized.

By *J O H N.B U N Y A N.*

CHAPTER I: THE HOUSE OF THE FOREST OF LEBANON

As Solomon built a house for Pharaoh's daughter, and that called the temple of the Lord; so he built a house in Lebanon, called "the house of the forest of Lebanon" (1 Kings 7:2).

Some, I perceive, have thought that this house, called "the house of the forest of Lebanon," was none other than that called the temple at Jerusalem, and that that was called "The house of the forest of Lebanon," because built of the wood that grew there. But that Solomon built another than that, even one in Lebanon, called "the house of the forest of Lebanon," is evident, and that from these reasons:—

First, That in the forest of Lebanon is mentioned as another, besides that called the temple of the Lord; and that too when the temple and its finishing is spoken of; yea, it is mentioned with an "also," as an additional house, besides the temple of the Lord.

"In the fourth year," saith the text, "was the foundation of the house of the Lord laid in the month Zif; and in the eleventh year in the month Bul, which is the eighth month, was the house finished throughout all the parts thereof, and according to all the fashion of it; so he was seven years in building it." "But Solomon was building his own house thirteen years, and he finished all his house. He built also the house of the forest of Lebanon," &c. (1 Kings 6:37,38; 7:1,2).

Can there now be any thing more plain? Is not here the house of the forest of Lebanon mentioned as another besides the temple? he built the temple, he built his own house, he built also the house of the forest of Lebanon.

Second. It is evident by the difference of their measures and dimensions. The length of the temple was threescore cubits; but the length of the house of the forest of Lebanon was an hundred cubits; so that the house of the forest of Lebanon was forty cubits more than was that called Solomon's temple: The breadth of Solomon's temple was twenty cubits, but the breadth of the house of the forest of Lebanon was fifty cubits: And as there is odds between threescore and fivescore, so there is also between twenty and fifty.

As to their height, they were both alike; but equality in height can no more make them the same, than can a twenty years' age in two, make them one and the same person.

Their porches also differed greatly; the porch of the temple was in length but twenty cubits, but the length of that of the house of the forest of Lebanon was fifty cubits. So that here also is thirty odds. The porch of the temple was but ten cubits broad; but the porch of the house of the forest of Lebanon thirty cubits. Now, I say, who that considereth these disproportions, can conclude that the house of the forest of Lebanon was none other than that called the temple of Jerusalem. For all this compare 1 Kings 6:2, 3 with 7:2, 6.

Third. If you add to these the different makes of the houses, it will sufficiently appear that they were not one. The house of the forest of Lebanon was built upon four rows of cedar pillars; but we read of no such pillars upon which the temple stood. The windows of the house of the forest of Lebanon stood in three rows, light against light; but we read of no such thing in the temple. The temple had two pillars before the door of its porch, but we read not of them before the door of the porch of the house of the forest of Lebanon. In the sixth and seventh chapters of the first book of Kings, these two houses, as to their make, are exactly set forth; so that he that listeth may search and see, if as to this I have not said the truth.

CHAPTER II: OF WHAT THE HOUSE OF THE FOREST OF LEBANON WAS A TYPE

T hat the house of the forest of Lebanon was a house significant, I think is clear; also, if it had not, we should not have had so particular an account thereof in the holy Word of God: I read but of four buildings wherein, in a particular manner, the houses or fabrics are, as to their manner of building, distinctly handled. The tabernacle is one, the temple another; the porch which he built for his throne, his throne for judgment; and this house of the forest of Lebanon is the fourth. Now the three first, to wit, the tabernacle, the temple, the porch and throne, wise men will say are typical; and therefore so is this.

[First.] I will therefore take it for granted that the house of the forest of Lebanon is a significative thing, yea, a figure of the church, as the temple at Jerusalem was, though not under the same consideration. The temple was a figure of the church under the gospel, as she relateth to worship; but the house of the forest of Lebanon was a figure of that church as she is assaulted for her worship, as she is persecuted for the same. Or take it more expressly thus: I take this house of the forest of Lebanon to be a type of the church in the wilderness, or as she is in her sackcloth state.

We read, before this house was built, that there was a church in the wilderness; and also, after this house was demolished, that there would be a church in the wilderness (Acts 7:38; Rev 12:14). But we now respect that wilderness state that the church of the New Testament is in, and conclude that this house of the forest of Lebanon was a type and figure of that; that is, of her wilderness state. And, methinks, the very place where this house was built does intimate such a thing; for this house was not built in a town, a city, &c., as was that called the temple of the Lord, but was built in a kind of a wood, a wilderness; it was built in the forest of Lebanon, unto which that saying seems directly to answer. "And to the woman," the church, "were given two wings of a great eagle, that she might fly into the wilderness into her place" (Rev 12:14). A wilderness state is a desolate, a tempted, an afflicted, a persecuted state (Jer 2:6). All which is more than intimated by the witnesses wearing of, and prophesying in sackcloth, and also expressed of by that Revelation 12.

Answerable to this is that of the prophet concerning this house of the forest of Lebanon, where he says, "Open thy doors, O Lebanon! that the fire may devour thy cedars." And again, "Howl, fir-tree; for the cedar is fallen" (Zech 11:1,2). What can be more express? The prophet here knocks at the very door of the house of the forest of Lebanon, and tells her that her cedars are designed for fire; unto which also most plainly answer the flames to which so many of the cedars of Lebanon, God's saints, I mean, for many hundred years, have been delivered for their profession; and by which, as another prophet has it, for many days they have fallen (Dan 11:33). Also when the king of Assyria came up with his army against Jerusalem, this was his vaunting, "I am come - to the sides of Lebanon, and I will cut down the tall cedars thereof" (Isa 37:24).

What was this king of Assyria but a type of the beast made mention of in the New Testament? Now, saith he, I will cut down the cedars of Lebanon; who are, in our gospel times, the tall ones of the church of God. And I say again, in that he particularly mentions Lebanon, he intends that house which Solomon built there, the which was built as a fortification to defend the religion of the temple, as the saints now in the wilderness of the people are set for the defence of the gospel. But more of this anon.

This house therefore was built to make assaults, and to be assaulted, as the church in the wilderness is; and hence the state of this house is compared to the condition of a woman in travail, struggling with her pains, as also we find the state of the church in the wilderness is—"O inhabitant of Lebanon, that makest thy nest in the cedars, how gracious shalt thou be when pangs come upon thee, the pain as of a woman in travail!" (Jer 22:23). And again, "Verily, verily, I say unto you, That ye shall weep and lament," and have sorrow, as a woman in travail (John 16:20-22). Much answering her case who, in her travails, and while "pained to be delivered," was said even in this case to stand before the dragon, who with open mouth sought to destroy her fruit, so "soon as it was born" (Rev 12:1-6).

Hence, again, when Christ calls his spouse out to suffer, he calls or draws her out of his house in Lebanon, to look "from the lions' dens, from the mountains of the leopards," to the things that are invisible; even as Paul said when he was in affliction, "We look not at the things which are seen" (Cant 4:8; 2 Cor 4:18). He draws them out thence, I say, as sheep appointed for the slaughter; yea, he goeth before them, and they follow him thither.

Also, when the prophet foretells the affliction of the church, he expresses it by the fall of the cedars of Lebanon, saying, The Lord shall cut down the thickets of the forest with iron; a little afore called the axe and saw. And Lebanon shall fall by a mighty one (Isa 10:15,34). And again, "The earth mourneth and languisheth: Lebanon is ashamed and hewn down" (Isa 33:9).

Do we think that the prophet prophesieth here against trees, against the natural cedars of Lebanon? No, no, it is a prophecy touching the afflicted state of the church in the wilderness, of which Lebanon, I mean this house of the forest of Lebanon, was a figure.

When God also threateneth the enemies of his church in the wilderness with his judgments, for their cruel dealing with her in the day of her desertion, he calls those judgments the violence of Lebanon. That is, by way of comparison, such as the violence done to Lebanon was. "The violence of Lebanon shall cover thee; and the spoil of beasts which made them [Lebanon] afraid, because of men's blood, and for the violence of the land, of the city, and of all that dwell therein" (Habb 2:17). This is like that, "Reward her, even as she rewarded you, and double unto her double according to her works" (Rev 18:6). This the church doth by her prayers. "The violence done to me and to my flesh be upon Babylon, shall the inhabitant of Zion say; and my blood upon the inhabitants of Chaldea, shall Jerusalem say" (Jer 51:35). And then shall be fulfilled that which is written, Look what they did unto Lebanon shall be done unto them (Oba 15; Eze 35:14,15).

God has his time to return the evil that the enemies do to his church, and he will do it when his time is come upon their own head; and this return is called the covering of them with the violence of Lebanon, or that violence showed to her in the day of her distress. It is yet further evident that this house of the forest of Lebanon was a type of the church in the wilderness:—

1. For that she is called a tower, or place of fortification and defence; the same term that is given to the church in a captivated state (Can 7:4; Micah 4:8-10). For as the church in the wilderness is compared to a woman in travail, to show her fruitfulness to God-ward in her most afflicted condition; so she is called a tower, to show her fortitude and courage, for God and his truth, against antichrist. I say therefore, unto both these is she compared in that scripture last cited, the which you may peruse if you please. A tower is a place of receipt for the afflicted, and so is the church under the rage of antichrist; yea, and though it is the only place designed by the enemy for ruin and destruction, yet it is the only place of safety in the world.

2. This tower, this house of the forest of Lebanon, it seems to be so built as to confront Damascus, the chief city of the king of Assyria; and in so doing it was a most excellent type of the spirit and design of the church in the wilderness, who is raised up, and built to confront antichrist. Hence Christ calls some of the features of his church, and compares them to this. "Thy neck," says he "is as a tower of ivory; thine eyes like the fish-pools in Heshbon, by the gate of Bath-rabbim; thy nose is as the tower of Lebanon which looketh toward Damascus" (Cant 7:4).

Thy nose, that great ornament of thy lovely countenance, is as a tower looking that way; so set, as Christ says of his, as a flint. And this is a comely feature in the church, that her nose stands like a tower, or as he says in another place, like a fenced brazen wall against Damascus, the metropolitan of her enemy: "for the head of Syria is Damascus" (Isa 7:8).

And as Christ thus compares his church, so she again returns, or compares the face of her Lord to the same, saying, "His legs are as pillars of marble, set upon sockets of fine gold: his countenance is as Lebanon, excellent as the cedars" (Can 5:15). Thus in Lebanon, in this brave house, is found the excellency of the church, and the beauty of Christ, for that they are both as a rock, with glory and majesty, bended against the enemies of the truth. "The face of the Lord is against them that do evil." Pillars his legs are here compared to, and pillars were they that upheld this house, this tower, which thus bravely was built with its face confronting the enemy's country.

Second. That this house of the forest of Lebanon was a type of the church in affliction, yet further appears, for that at the fall of Babylon her cedars are said to rejoice in special. "The fir-trees rejoice at thee, and the cedars of Lebanon, saying, Since thou art laid down, no feller is come up against us" (Isa 14:8). This is at the destruction of Babylon, the type of that called antichrist.

But why should Lebanon, the cedars in Lebanon, in an especial manner here, be said to rejoice at his downfall: doubtless to show that as the enemy made his inroad upon Jerusalem; so in a particular manner Lebanon, and the house there, were made to smoke for it (Isa 37:24; Jer 22:23; Zech 11:1). This answereth to that, "Rejoice over her thou heaven; and ye holy apostles and prophets, for God hath avenged you of her." Hence again, when he speaks of giving glory to his afflicted church, for all the sorrow which she hath sustained in her bearing witness for the truth against antichrist, he calls it the glory of Lebanon. That is, as I take it, the glory that belongs to her, for the afflictions which she underwent for his name. "The glory of Lebanon shall be given unto it" (Isa 35:2). And again, "The glory of Lebanon shall come unto thee" (Isa 60:13). These are promises to the church for her suffering of affliction, and they are made unto her as she bears the name of Lebanon, who or which was her type in those havocs made in it, when the enemy, as I said, assaulted the church of old.

Thus by these few lines I have showed you that there was a similitude betwixt this house in the forest of Lebanon, and our gospel church in the wilderness. Nor need we stumble because this word house is not subjoined in every particular place, where this sorrow or joy of Lebanon is made mention of; for it is an usual thing with the Holy Ghost, when he directs his speech to a man, to speak as if he spake to a tree; and when he directs his voice to a king, to speak as if he intended the kingdom; so when he speaks of the house, to speak as to the forest of Lebanon. Instances many might be given.

CHAPTER III: OF THE LARGENESS OF THE HOUSE OF THE FOREST OF LEBANON

The house of the forest of Lebanon was forty cubits longer than was the temple at Jerusalem, to show that the church in the wilderness would increase more, and be far larger than she that had peace and prosperity. And as it was forty cubits longer, so it was thirty cubits wider, still showing that every way she would abound. Hence they that came out of great tribulation, when compared with others, are said to be a numberless number, or a multitude which no man could number, of all nations, and kindreds, and people, and tongues. "These," saith one, "are they which came out of the great tribulation, and have washed their robes, and made them white in the blood of the Lamb; therefore are they before the throne of God" (Rev 7:14,15).

The church, as it respected temple-worship, was confined to the land of Canaan; but our New Testament persecuted one is scattered among the nations, as a flock of sheep are scattered in a wood or wilderness. Hence they are said to be in "the wilderness of the people," fitly answering to this house of the forest of Lebanon (Eze 20:35-37).

But though the house exceeded in length and breadth the temple of Jerusalem, yet as to their height they were the same, to show that what acts that in the wilderness doth, above what they have been capable to do, that have not been in that condition; yet the nature of their grace is the same (Rom 15:27; 1 Peter 1:1).

But, I say, as for length and breadth, the church in the wilderness exceeds more than the house of the forest of Lebanon did that of the temple at Jerusalem, as it is written; "More are the children of the desolate than the children of the married wife, saith the Lord." And again: "Thou shalt break forth on the right hand and on the left; and thy seed shall inherit the Gentiles, and make the desolate cities to be inhabited" (Isa 54:1-3). This is spoken of the church in the wilderness, that was made up chiefly of the Gentiles, of which the house of the forest of Lebanon was a figure; and how she at last shall recover herself from the yoke and tyranny of antichrist. And then she shall shoulder it with her adversary, saying, "Give place to me, that I may dwell" (Isa 49:20).

And I will add, it was not only thus magnificent for length and breadth, but for terror; it was compacted after the manner of a castle, or stronghold, as was said before. It was a tower built for an armoury, for Solomon put there his two hundred targets and three hundred shields of gold (2 Chron 9:15,16). This place therefore was a terror to the heathen, on that side of the church especially, because she stood with her nose so formidable against Damascus: no marvel therefore if the implacable cried out against them, Help, "men of Israel, help!" And, "Will ye rebel against the king?" (Acts 21:28; Neh 2:19).

For it is the terror, or majesty and fortitude, which God has put upon the church in the wilderness, that makes the Gentiles so bestir them to have her under foot. Besides, they misapprehend concerning her, as if she was for destroying kings, for subverting kingdoms, and for bringing all to desolation, and so they set themselves against her, "crying, These that have turned the world upside down are come hither also; whom Jason hath received: and these all do contrary to the decrees of Caesar, saying that there is another king, one Jesus" (Acts 17:5-7). Indeed, the very name of Jesus is the very tower of the Christian church, and that by which she frights the world, but not designedly, but through their misunderstanding; for neither she, nor her Jesus, is for doing them any hurt; however, this is that which renders her yet in their eye "terrible as an army with banners" (Cant 6:10). How then could she escape persecution for a time, for it was the policy of Jeroboam (1 Kings 12:26-28). And it is yet the policy of the nations to secure themselves against this their imagined danger, and therefore to use all means, as Pharaoh did, to keep this people low enough, saying, "Come on, let us deal wisely with them, lest they multiply, and it come to pass that when there falleth out any war, they join also to our enemies, and fight against us, and so get them up out of the land" (Exo 1:10).

But could the house of Lebanon, though a fortified place, assault Damascus? Could it remove from the place on which God had set it? It only was a place of defence for Judah, or for the worship of the temple. And had the adversary let the temple-worship and worshippers alone, the shields and targets in the house of the forest of Lebanon had not been uncovered, had not been made bare against them. The same may now be said of the church in the wilderness, she moveth no sedition, she abideth in her place; let her temple-worshippers but alone, and she will be as if she were not in the world; but if you afflict her, "Fire proceedeth out of their mouth and devoureth their enemies; and if any man will hurt them, he must in this manner be killed" (Rev 11:5). And so die by the sword of the Spirit. But because the weapons of the church, though none of them are carnal, be so talked of in the world, the blind are yet more afraid of her than they in this manner are like to be hurt by her, and therefore they of old have peeled, and polled, and endeavoured to spoil her all along, sending their servants, and saying to their bailiffs and sheriffs, "Go - to a nation scattered and peeled, to a people terrible from their beginning, - a nation meted out and trodden down, whose land the rivers have spoiled!" (Isa 18:2). But this people shall prevail, though not by worldly force; her God will deliver her. And then, or at "that time, shall the present be brought to the Lord of hosts of a people scattered and peeled, and from a people terrible from their beginning hitherto; a nation meted out and trodden under foot, whose land the rivers have spoiled, to the place of the name of the Lord of hosts, the Mount Zion" (Isa 18:7).

Now thus did the house of the forest of Lebanon provoke; it was built defensively, it had a tower, it had armour; its tower confronted the enemy's land. No marvel then, if the king of Assyria so threatened to lay his army on the sides of Lebanon and to cut down the tall cedars thereof (Isa 37:24).

The largeness, therefore, and prowess of the church, by reason of her inherent fortitude and the valorous acts that she hath done by suffering, by prayer, by faith, and a constant enduring of hardship for the truth, doth force into the world a belief, through their own guilt and clamours of conscience against them for their debaucheries, that this house of the forest of Lebanon will destroy them all when she shall be delivered from her servitude. "Come now, therefore," saith Balak to Balaam, and "curse me this people," if peradventure I may overcome them: when he might have let them pass peaceably by, and they would not have lifted up a finger against him. Wherefore, from all these things it appears that the house of the forest of Lebanon was a type of the church in the wilderness.

CHAPTER IV: OF THE MATERIALS OF WHICH THE HOUSE OF THE FOREST OF LEBANON WAS MADE

The foundation of the house of the forest of Lebanon was of the same great stones which were laid in the foundation of the temple of the Lord (1 Kings 7:2-11). And this shows that the church in the wilderness has the same foundation and support as had the temple that was at Jerusalem, though in a state of sackcloth, tears, and affliction, the lot of the church in the wilderness; for she, while there, is to howl (Zech 11:2). Now since the foundation is the same, what is it but to show also that she, though in an afflicted condition, shall certainly stand; "The gates of hell shall not prevail against it" (Matt 16:18). Her confronting idolatrous nations is therefore a sign of her troubles, not any prediction of a fall. Her rock is steadfast, not like the rock of her adversaries, the enemy being judges (Deut 32:31).

But that which in special I take notice of is, that I find, in a manner, in this house of the forest of Lebanon, nothing but pillars, and beams, great timber, and thick beams, and of those was the house builded; pillars to hold up, and thick beams to couple together, and thus was the house finished. I read not here of any garnishing, either of the pillars, beams, doors, posts, walls, or any part of the house; all was plain, without garnish, fitly representing the state of the church in the wilderness, which was clothed with sackcloth, covered with ashes, wearing her mourning weeds, with her tears upon her cheeks, and a yoke or band about her neck (Isa 52:1,2, 61:3).

By this kind of description we may also note with what kind of members this house, this church is furnished. Here, as I said, that is, in the house of the forest of Lebanon, you find pillars, pillars, so in the church in the wilderness. O the mighty ones of which this church was compacted! they were all pillars, strong, bearing up the house against wind and weather; nothing but fire and sword could dissolve them. As therefore this house was made up of great timber, so this church in the wilderness was made up of giants in grace. These men had the faces of lions; no prince, no king, no threat, no terror, no torment, could make them yield; they loved not their lives unto the death. They have laughed their enemies in the face, they have triumphed in the flames.

They were pillars, they were pillars of cedar: the cedar is the highest tree in the world; wherefore in that this house was made of cedar, it may be to denote that in the church in the wilderness, however contemned by men, was the highest perfection of goodness, as of faith, love, prayer, holy conversation, and affection for God and his truth. For indeed none ever showed the like, none ever showed higher cedars than those that were in Lebanon. None ever showed higher saints than were they in the church in the wilderness. Others talked, these have suffered; others have said, these have done; these have voluntarily taken their lives in their hands, for they loved them not to the death; and have fairly, and in cool blood, laid them down before the world, God, angels, and men, for the confirming of the truth which they have professed (Acts 15:26; Rev 12:11). These are pillars, these are strong ones indeed. It is meet, therefore, that the church in the wilderness, since she was to resemble the house of the forest of Lebanon, should be furnished with these mighty ones.

Cedars! the same that the holiest of all in the temple was covered within, and that house was a figure of heaven, to show that the church of God in the wilderness, how base and low soever in the judgment of the world, is yet the only heaven that God hath among the children of men. Here are many nations, many kingdoms, many countries, and many cities, but the church in the wilderness was but one, and she was the heaven that God has here; hence she is called, "Thou heaven. Rejoice over her thou heaven" (Rev 18:20). And again, when the combustion for religion is in the church in the wilderness it is said to be in heaven—"And there was war in heaven. Michael and his angels fought against the dragon; and the dragon fought, and his angels" (Rev 12:7).

The church therefore loseth not all her titles of honour, no, not when at the lowest, she is God's heaven still; though she may not be called now a crown of glory, yet she is still God's lily amongst thorns; though she may not be called the church of Jerusalem, yet she may the church in the wilderness; and though she may not be called Solomon's temple, yet she may the house of the forest of Lebanon. Cedars! cedars are tall and sweet, and so are the members of the church in the wilderness. O their smell, their scent, it hath been "as the wine of Lebanon" (Hosea 14:5-7). They that have gone before have left this smell still in the nostrils of their survivors, as that both fragrant and precious.

This house of the forest of Lebanon was builded "upon four rows of cedar pillars" (1 Kings 7:2). These four rows were the bottom pillars, those upon which the whole weight of the house did bear. The Holy Ghost saith here four rows, but says not how many were in a row. But we will suppose them to allude to the twelve apostles, or to the apostles and prophets, upon whose foundation the church in the wilderness is said to be built (Eph 2:20). And if so, then it shows that as the house of the forest of Lebanon stood upon these four rows of pillars, as the names of the twelve tribes stood in four rows of precious stones upon Aaron's breastplate when he went into the holiest, so this house, or church in the wilderness, stands upon the doctrine of the apostles and prophets (Exo 28:17, 29:10). But because it only saith it stood upon four rows, not specifying any number, therefore as to this we may say nothing certain, yet I think such a conjecture hath some show of truth in it, however, I will leave it to wiser judgments.

"And it was covered with cedar above, upon the beams that lay on forty-five pillars, fifteen in a row" (1 Kings 7:3). These pillars, as the others, are such upon which the house did also bear; this is clear, because the beams that lay upon the four rows of pillars afore-mentioned lay also upon these forty-five.

It seems, therefore, that these four rows of pillars were they that were the more outside ones; that is, two rows on this side of the house and two rows also on that; and that those forty-five pillars, fifteen in a row, stood in three rows more inward, and so did bear up with the other the beams that were laid upon them, much like to those inner pillars that usually stand in our parish churches. If so, then the first four rows did seem to be a guard to these, for that, as they stood more to the outsides of the house, so more to the weather, and nearer to the first approach of the enemy.

And this may show that the apostles in their doctrine are not only a foundation to the forty-five pillars, but a protection and defence; I say a protection and defence to all the pillars that ever were besides in the church in the wilderness. And it is to be considered that the four rows are mentioned as placed first, and so were those upon which the thick beams that first were for coupling of the house were laid; the which most fitly teacheth that the office and graces of the apostles were first in the church in the wilderness, according to 1 Corinthians 12:18.

These forty-five pillars standing in the midst, by the others, may also be to show that in the time of the trouble of the church in her wilderness state, there will be those that will stand by and maintain her apostolical doctrine, though for so doing they bear the burthen of the whole. But I read of no chambers for ease or rest in this house, here is no room for chambering. They that were for being members in the church in the wilderness, must not look for rest until their Lord shall come (Rom 13:13,14; 2 Thess 1:5-9).

Here therefore was but hard lodging; the house of the forest of Lebanon was not made for tender skins and for those that cannot lie out of down beds, but for those that were war-like men, and that were willing to endure hardness for that religion that God had set up in his temple, and is fitly answered by that of the apostle: "Thou, therefore," my son, "endure hardness as a good soldier of Jesus Christ. No man that warreth entangleth himself with the affairs of this life, that he may please him who hath chosen him to be a soldier" (2 Tim 2:3,4). Forty-five pillars! It was forty-five years that the church was of old in a bewildered and warlike condition before she enjoyed her rest in Canaan (Josh 14:10). Now, as there were forty-five years of trouble, so here are forty-five pillars for support, perhaps to intimate that God will have in his church in the wilderness a sufficient succession of faithful men that, like pillars, shall bear up the truth above water all the time of Antichrist's reign and rage.

The thick beams that lay over-thwart to couple this house of the forest of Lebanon together, did bear upon these forty-five pillars, to show that, by the burden-bearers that have and shall be in the church of God in the wilderness, the unity of that house is through the Spirit maintained. And indeed, had it not been for these pillars, the sufferers, these burden-bearers in the church, our house in the forest of Lebanon, or, more properly, our church in the wilderness, had before this been but in a poor condition. Thus therefore this church, which in her time is the pillar and ground of truth in the world, has been made to stand and abide it. "When the blast of the terrible ones has been as a storm against the wall" (Isa 25:4; 1 Tim 3:15). "Many a time have they afflicted me from my youth, may Israel now say: many a time have they afflicted me from my youth: yet they have not prevailed against me" (Psa 129:1,2).

Thus you see how the house of the forest of Lebanon was a type of the church in the wilderness; and you see also by this the reason why the house of the forest of Lebanon had its inward glory lying more in great pillars and thick beams than in other ornaments. And indeed, here had need be pillars and pillars and beams and beams too, since it was designed for assaults to be made upon it, since it was set for a butt for the marksman, and to be an object for furious heathens to spend their rage against its walls.

The glory therefore of the temple lay in one thing, and the glory of this house lay in another: the glory of the temple lay in that she contained the true form and modes of worship, and the glory of the house of the forest of Lebanon lay in her many pillars and thick beams, by which she was made capable, through good management, to give check to those of Damascus when they should attempt to throw down that worship.

And as I said before, these pillars were sweet-scented pillars, for that they were made of cedar; but what cared the enemy for that, they were offensive to him, for that they were placed as a fortification against him. Nor is it any allurement to Satan to favour the mighty ones in the church in the wilderness for the fragrant smell of their sweet graces, nay, both he and his angels are the more bent to oppose them because they are so sweet-scented. The cedars therefore got nothing because they were cedars at the hands of the barbarous Gentiles—for they would burn the cedars—as the angels or pillars get nothing of favour at the hands of Antichrist because they are pillars of and angels for the truth, yea, they so much the more by her are abhorred. Well, but they are pillars for all that, yea, pillars to the church in the wilderness, as the others were in the house of the forest of Lebanon, and pillars they will abide there, dead and alive, when the enemy has done what he can.

The pillars were set in three rows, for so are forty-five when they are set fifteen in a row. And they were set in three rows to bear. This manner also of their standing thus was also doubtless significant. But again, they, these pillars, may be set, or placed thus in three rows in the house of the forest of Lebanon, to show that the three offices of Christ are the great things that the church in the wilderness must bear up before the world.

The three offices of Christ, they are his priestly, his prophetical, and his kingly offices. These are those in which God's glory and the church's salvation are most immediately concerned, and they that have been most opposed by the devil and his angels. All heresies, errors, and delusions with which Christ's church has been assaulted in all ages, have bent themselves against some one or all of these (Rev 16:13,16). Christ is a priest to save, a prophet to teach, and a king to rule his church (Isa 33:22). But this Antichrist cannot bear, therefore he attempts to get up into the throne himself, and to act as if he were one above all that is called God, or that is worshipped (2 Thess 2:3,4; Rev 19:19-21). But behold! here are pillars in three rows, mighty pillars to bear up Christ in these his offices before the world and against all falsehood and deceit.

Fifteen in a row, I can say no further than I can see; what the number of fifteen should signify I know not, God is wiser than man; but yet methinks their standing thus should signify a reserve; as suppose the first three that the enemy comes at should be destroyed by their hands, there are three times fourteen behind; suppose again that they should serve the next three so, yet there is a reserve behind. When that fine one, Jezebel, had done what she could against the afflicted church in her time, yet there was left a reserve, a reserve of seven thousand that were true worshippers of God (1 Kings 19:18; Rom 11:4).

Always when Antichrist made his inroads upon the church in the wilderness, to slay, to cut off, and to kill, yet some of the pillars stood, they were not all burnt in the fire, nor cut down. They said indeed, "Come and let us cut them off from being a nation, that the name of Israel may be no more in remembrance" (Psa 83:4). But what then? there is a difference betwixt saying and doing; the bush was not therefore consumed because it was set on fire; the church shall not be consumed although she be afflicted (Exo 3:3). And this reason is, because God has still his fifteens; therefore if Abel falls by the hand of Cain, Seth is put in his place (Gen 4:25). If Moses is taken away, Joshua shall succeed him (Josh 1:2,3). And if the devil break the neck of Judas, Matthias is at hand to take his office (Acts 1:16-26). God has, I say, a succession of pillars in his house; he has to himself a reserve.

Yet again, methinks that there should be forty-five pillars, and besides them four rows of pillars, and all this to bear up an invisible burden, for we read of nothing upon the pillars but the heavens and roof. It should be to show that it is impossible that a carnal heart should conceive of the weight that truth lays upon the conscience of a believer. They see, nothing, alas, nothing at all, but a beam, a truth, and, say they, are you such fools to stand groaning to bear up that, or what is contained therein? They, I say, see not the weight, the glory, the weight of glory that is in a truth of God, and therefore they laugh at them that will count it worth the while to endure so much to support it from falling to the ground. Great pillars and beams, great saints and great truths, are in the church of God in the wilderness; and the beams lie upon the pillars, or the truth upon the saints.

The tabernacle and ark formerly were to be borne upon men's shoulders, even as these great beams are borne up by these pillars. And as this tabernacle and ark were to be carried hither and thither, according to the appointment of God, so were these beams to be by these pillars borne up, that therewith the house might be girt together, kept uniform, and made to stand fast, notwithstanding the wind and storm.

CHAPTER V: OF THE WINDOWS IN THE HOUSE OF THE FOREST OF LEBANON

The house of the forest of Lebanon had many windows in it; "And there were windows in three rows, and light was against light in three ranks" (1 Kings 7:4). Windows are to let the light in at, and the eye out at, to objects at a distance from the house, and from those that are therein.

The windows here are figures of the Word of God, by which light the light of life is let into the heart; through that, the glass of these windows, the beams of the Sun of righteousness shine into the church. Hence the word is compared to glass, through which the glorious face of Christ is seen (2 Cor 3:18). This, therefore, this house of the forest of Lebanon had; it had windows, a figure of that Word of God, through, and by which, the church in the wilderness sees the mind of God, and so what while there she ought to believe, do, and leave undone in the world.

This house had plenty of windows—three rows of windows on both sides the house. In three rows; by these windows in three rows perhaps was prefigured how into the church in the wilderness was to shine the doctrine of the Trinity: yea, to signify that she was to be possessed with that in her most low state, and when under her greatest clouds. The doctrine of the Trinity! that is the substance, that is the ground and fundamental of all (1 John 2:22,23, 4:2-4; 2 John 9,10). For by this doctrine, and by this only, the man is made a Christian; and he that has not this doctrine, his profession is not worth a button. You must know that sometimes the church in the wilderness has but little light, but the diminution of her light is not then so much in or as to substantials, as it is as to circumstantial things; she has then the substantials with her, in her darkest day, even windows in three rows.

The doctrine of the Trinity! You may ask me what that is? I answer. It is that doctrine that showeth us the love of God the Father, in giving of his Son: the love of God the Son, in giving of himself; and the love of the Lord the Spirit, in his work of regenerating of us, that we may be made able to lay hold of the love of the Father by his Son, and so enjoy eternal life by grace. This doctrine was always let in at these windows into the church in the wilderness, for to make her sound in faith, and hearty in obedience; as also meek and patient in temptation and tribulation. And as to the substance of Christianity, this doctrine is sufficient for any people, because it teaches faith, and produceth a good moral life. These therefore, if these doctrines shine upon us, through these windows of heaven, so as that we see them, and receive them, they make us fit to glorify God here, and meet to be glorified of, and with him hereafter. These lights, therefore, cause that the inhabitants of this church in the wilderness see their way through the dark pitch night of this world. For as the house of the forest of Lebanon, this church of God in the wilderness had always her lights, or windows in these three rows, to guide, to solace, and comfort her.

This house therefore, is thus discriminated and distinguished from all other houses in the world; no house, that we read of in the Bible, was thus adorned with light, or had windows in three rows, but this; and answerable hereunto, no congregation or church, but the true church of God, has the true antitype thereof. Light! windows! A sufficiency of windows was of great use to a people that dwelt in a forest, or wood, as the inhabitants of the house of the forest of Lebanon did. But how solitary had this house been, had it had no light at all! To be in a wood, and that without windows, is one of the worst of conditions. This also is the relief that the church in the wilderness had; true, she was in a wood, but had light, called in another place God's rod, or his Word, which giveth instruction. "Feed thy people with thy rod, the flock of thine heritage, which dwell solitary in the wood," &c. (Micah 7:14).

To be, as was said, in a wood, and without light too, is a condition very desolate: the Egyptians found it so, for all they were in their houses (Exo 10:21,23). But how much more then is that people's case to be lamented that are under persecution, but have not light in three rows to guide them. But this is not the state of the church in the wilderness; she has her windows in three rows, to wit, the light of the face of the Father, the light of the face of the Son, and the light of the face of the Holy Ghost; all shining through the windows or glass of the Word, to her comfort and consolation, though now in the forest of Lebanon.

"And light was against light in three ranks." This is an additional account of the windows that were in the house of the forest of Lebanon. Before he said she had windows in three rows, but now he adds that there was light against light, light opposite to light, and that also in three ranks. In that he saith they were in ranks, he either means in order, or insinuates a military posture, for in both these ways is this word taken (Num 2:16,24; 1 Chron 12:33,38; Mark 6:40). Nor need any smile because I say the lights were set in a military posture; we read of potsherds striving with potsherds; and why may it not as well be said, "light was against light" (Isa 45:9).

But we will pursue our design. Here is opposition insinuated; in the margin it is "sight against sight"; wherefore the lights thus placed in the house of the forest of Lebanon give me another encouragement, to think that this house was a type of the church in the wilderness, and that she is the seat of spiritual war also (Rev 12:7). For as this house of the forest of Lebanon was that which was the object of the rage of the king of Assyria, because it stood in his way to hinder his ruining Jerusalem; so the spirit and faithfulness of the church of God in the wilderness stands in the way, and hinders Antichrist's bringing of the truth to the ground.

And as the enemy brake into Lebanon, and did set fire to her cedars, so the boar, the Antichrist, the dragon, and his angels, got into the church in the wilderness (Psa 80:13; 2 Thess 2:4; Rev 12:7). This being so, here must needs be war; and since the war is not carnal but spiritual, it must be made by way of controversy, contention, disputation, argument, reasonings, &c. which were the effect of opposite apprehensions, fitly set out in this house of the forest of Lebanon, for that there was "light against light," "sight against sight," in three ranks. Wherefore in that he saith "light was against light in three ranks," he suggesteth, to the life, how it would be in the church in the wilderness. And suppose they were the truly godly that made the first assault, can they be blamed? For who can endure a boar in a vineyard; a man of sin in a holy temple; or a dragon in heaven? What then if the church made the first assault? Who bid the boar come there? What had he to do in God's house? The church, as the house of the forest of Lebanon, would have been content with its own station; and bread and water will serve a man, that may with peace enjoy his delights in other things. But when privilege, property, life, delight, heaven, and salvation, comes to be intruded, no marvel if the woman, though but a woman, cries out, and set her light against them; had she seen the thief, and said nothing, she had been far worse.

I told you before that by the windows is meant the Word, which is compared to glass (1 Cor 13:12; 2 Cor 3:18; James 1:23-25). What, then, is the Word against the Word? No, verily, it is therefore not the Word, but opposite apprehensions thereabout, that the Holy Ghost now intends; for he saith not that window was against window, respecting the true sense of the Word, but light was against light, respecting the divers notions and apprehensions that men of opposite spirits would have about the Word. Nor are we to take this word light, especially in the antitype, in a proper but in a metaphorical sense, that is, with respect to the judgment of both parties. Here is the true church, and she has the true light; here also is the boar, the man of sin, and the dragon; and they see by their way, and yet, as I said, all by the self-same windows. They that are the church do, in God's light, see light; but they that are not, do in their own way see. And let a man, and a beast, look out at the same window, the same door, the same casement, yet the one will see like a man, and the other but like a beast. No marvel then, though they have the same windows, that "light is against light," and sight against sight in this house. For there are that known nothing but what they know naturally as brutes (Psa 92:6; Jer 10:8,14,21; Jude 10).

No marvel then if there is here a disagreement; the beast can but see as a beast, but the church is resolved not to be guided by the eye of a beast, though he pretends to have his light by that very window by which the church has hers. The beast is moon-eyed, and puts darkness for light, yea, and hates the light that is so indeed; but the saints will not hear him, for they know the voice of their Lord (Isa 5:20; John 3:20). How then can it be but that light should be against light in this house, and that in a military posture? And how can it be but that here "every battle of the warrior" should be "with confused noise, and garments rolled in blood" (Isa 9:5).

And in that he saith, "light was against light in three ranks," it shows their preparations one against another; also that they on both sides are resolved to stand by their way. The church is confident, the man of sin is confident; they both have the same windows to see by, and so they manage their matters; yet not so simply by the windows, as by their divers judgments they make of that which shineth in at them. Each one therefore hath the true and false profession, will be confident of his own way; he that was right, knew he was right; and he that was wrong, thought he was right, and so the battle began. "There is a way that seemeth right unto a man, but the end thereof are the ways of death" (Prov 14:12).

Nor is it in man to help it; there has been reasoning, there has been disputing, there has blood also been spilt on both sides, through the confidence that each had of the goodness of his own way; but no reconciliation is made, the enmity is set here of God; iron and clay cannot mix (Gen 3:15; Dan 2:42,43). God will have things go on thus in the world, till his words shall be fulfilled: "The deceived, and the deceiver, are his" (Job 12:16). Things therefore must have their course in the church in the wilderness, till the mystery of God shall be fulfilled (Rev 17:17).

Hence it is said God will bring Gog against his people of Israel, "as a cloud to cover the land" (Eze 38:16). But for what cause? Why, that he may contend a while with them, and then fall by their light to the ground. Therefore he says also, that he "will give unto Gog a place there of graves in Israel, and it shall be called the valley of Hamon-gog" (Eze 39:11).

God will get himself great glory by permitting the boar, the man of sin, and the dragon, to revel it in the church of God; for they, by setting up and contending for their darkness and calling of it the light, and by setting of it against that light, which is light in very deed, do not only prove the power of truth where it is, but illustrate it so much the more. For as black sets off white, and darkness light, so error sets off truth. He that calls a man a horse, doth in conclusion but fix the belief of his humanity so much the more in the apprehension of all rational creatures.

"Light against light in three ranks." The three ranks on the church's side signify her light in the Trinity, as was said, and in the three offices of Christ; and the ranks against these three ranks be to signify the opposite apprehensions of the enemy. They differ also about the authority of the Word, and ordinances, about the offices, officers, and executions of office, in the church, &c. There is an opposition everywhere, even round about the house; there was "light against light in three ranks." This house of the forest of Lebanon was therefore a significative thing, wisely built and fit for the purpose for which it was designed, which was to show what afterward would be the state of the church in the wilderness. Nor could anything in the temple more aptly express itself in a typical way, as to any of the things concerning New Testament matters, than doth this house of the forest of Lebanon, as to the things designed to be signified thereby. It speaks, can we but hear: it points to things, as it were with a finger, have we but eyes to see.

It is not therefore to be wondered at that we hear both parties plead so much for their authority, crying out against each other, as those that destroy religion. So doth the church, so doth the man of sin. The living child is mine, saith one; nay, but the dead child is thine, and the living child is mine, says the other. And thus they spake before the king (1 Kings 3:16-22). Now this could not be, were there not different apprehensions here; light against light then is the cause of all this; and here is "light against light in three ranks"; and so will be until the beast is dead.

The church will not give place, for she knows she has the truth; the dragon and his angels, they will not give place, but as beaten back by the power of the truth; for thus it is said of the dragon and his angels, they fought and prevailed not. Therefore there will, there must, there cannot but be a spiritual warfare here, and that until one of the two are destroyed, and their body given to the burning flame (Dan 7:11; Rev 19:20).

CHAPTER VI: OF THE DOORS AND POSTS, AND THEIR SQUARE, WITH THE WINDOWS OF THE HOUSE OF THE FOREST OF LEBANON

"And all the doors and posts were square, with the windows." The doors, they were for entrance, the posts were the support of the doors, and the windows were, as was hinted before, for light. Now here they are said to be all square; square is a note of perfection; but this word square may be taken two ways. 1. Either as to the fashion of the things themselves; or, 2. With reference to the uniform order of the whole.

In the first sense was the altar of burnt-offering, the altar of incense, and the breastplate of judgment, square (Exo 27:1, 28:16; 30:2). And so also it is said of our New Testament New Jerusalem (Rev 21:16). But the square in the text is not thus to be understood, but if I mistake not, as is signified under the second head, that is for an uniform order. The whole fabric, as the doors, posts, and windows, presented themselves to beholders in an exact uniform order, and so right delectable to behold. Hence we may gather that this house of the forest of Lebanon was so exactly built, and consequently so complete to view, that it was alluring to the beholders; and that the more, for that so pretty a fabric should be found in a forest or wood. A lily among thorns, a pearl on a dunghill, and beauty under a veil, will make one turn aside to look on it.

Answerable to this, the church, even in the wilderness, or under persecution, is compared not only to a woman, but to a comely and delicate woman. And who, that shall meet such a creature in a wood, unless he feared God, but would seek to ravish and defile her.

Therefore I say, that which is here said to be square, must be understood to be so, as to prospect and view, or right taking to the eye.

Thus therefore they are allured, and think to defile her in the bed of love; but coming to her, and finding of her chaste, and filled with nothing but armour, and men at arms, to maintain her chastity, nolens volens—their fleshly love is turned into cruel rage, and so they go to variance.

"I have likened," says God, "The daughter of Zion to a comely and delicate woman" (Jer 6:2). But where is she? O! she is in the field, in the forest among the shepherds. But what will they do with her? Why, because she complies not with their desires, they "prepare war against her," saying, "Arise, let us go up at noon. Arise, and let us go by night, and let us destroy her palaces" (Jer 6:4,5). Wherefore the beauty of the house of the forest of Lebanon, as well as the fortitude thereof, was a temptation to the enemy to come to take it into their possession; especially since it stood, as it were, on the borders of Israel, and so faced the enemy's country.

Thus the church, though in her weeds of widowhood, is become the desire of the eyes of the nations; for indeed her features are such, considering who is her head, where mostly to the eye beauty lies, that whoso sees but the utmost glimpse of her, is easily ravished with her beauties. See how the prophet words it—"Many nations are gathered together against thee, that say, Let her be defiled, and let our eye look upon Zion" (Micah 4:11).

The church, the very name of the church of God, is beautiful in the world; and, as among women, she that has beauty has her head desired, if it might be, to stand upon another woman's shoulders; so this, and that, and every nation that beholds the beauty of the church, would fain be called by that name. The church, one would think, was but in a homely dress when she was coming out of captivity; and yet then the people of the countries desired to be one with her. "Let us [said they to Zerubbabel, and to the fathers of the church] build with you, for we seek your God as ye do" (Ezra 4:2).

The very name of the church, as I said, is striven for of the world, but that is the church which Christ has made so; her features also remain with herself, as this comely prospect of the house of the forest of Lebanon abode with it, whoever beheld or wished for it. The beauty therefore of this house, though it stood in the forest, was admirable; even as is the beauty of the church in the wilderness, though in a bewildered state.

Hear the relation that the Holy Ghost gives of the intrinsic beauty of the church, when she was to go to be in a persecuted state; she was "clothed with the sun, and the moon under her feet, and upon her head a crown of twelve stars" (Rev 12:1). And yet now the dragon stood by her (Rev 12:4). But I say, Here is a woman! let who will attempt it, show such another in the world, if he can.

They therefore that have any regard to morality, civility, or to ceremonial comeliness, covet to be of the church of God, or to appropriate that glorious title to themselves. And here, indeed, Antichrist came in; she took this name to herself; and though she could not come at the sun, nor moon, nor stars, to adorn herself with them, yet she has found something that makes her comely in her followers' eyes. See how the Holy Ghost sets her forth. She "was arrayed in purple and scarlet colour, and decked with gold and precious stones, and pearls, having a golden cup in her hand," &c. (Rev 17:4). Hence she is called, "The well- favoured harlot," "the lady of kingdoms," &c. (Nahum 3:4; Isa 47:5,7).

But because the chaste matron, the spouse of Christ, would not allow this slut to run away with this name, therefore she gets upon the back of her beast, and by him pushes this woman into the dirt; but because her faith and love to her husband remains, she turns again, and pleads by her titles, her features, and ornaments, that she, and she only, is she whose square answereth to the square of her figure, and to the character which her Lord hath given of his own, and so the game began. For so soon as this mistress became a dame in the world, and found that she had her stout abettors, she attempts to turn all things topsy-turvy, and to set them and to make of them what she lists. And now she will have an altar like that which was Tiglath-pileser's. Now must the Lord's brazen altar be removed from its place, the borders of the basis must be cut off, and the laver removed from off them; the molten sea must also now be taken off the backs of the brazen oxen, where Solomon set it, and be set on a pavement of stone (2 Kings 16:10-17).

Solomon! alas, Solomon's nobody now; this woman is wiser in her own conceit than seven men that can render a reason. Now also the covert for the Sabbath must be turned to the use of the king of Assyria, &c. (2 Kings 16:18). Thus has the beauty of God's church betrayed her into the hands of her lovers, who loved her for themselves, for the devil, and for the making of her a seat, a throne for the man of sin. And poor woman, all her struggling and striving, and crying out under the hands of these ravishers, has not, as yet, delivered her, though it has saved her life (Deut 22:25- 27).

But though thus it has been with Christ's true church, and will be as long as his enemy Antichrist reigns, yet the days will come when her God will give her her ornaments, and her bracelets, and her liberty, and her joy, that she had in the day of her espousals.

CHAPTER VII: OF THE REPETITION OF LIGHT AGAINST LIGHT IN THE HOUSE OF THE FOREST OF LEBANON

To be sure it was not superfluously done of the Holy Ghost to make repetition of these words, "And light was against light in three ranks," therefore something is intended in the adding of them again that was not intended by the first mentioning of them (1 Kings 7:4,5).

I have told you what I thought was intended by the first rehearsal of them, namely, to show how Antichrist got in with his sensuality, and opposed it to the true light of the Word of God, exalting himself above God, and also above all Divine revelation; this was his light against light. But, I say, why is it repeated? For he saith, "Light was against light in three ranks" again. Truly, I think it is repeated to show the evil effects the first antichristian opposition would have in the church of God, towards the end of her wilderness state. For, "light against light" now, for that it is here repeated, is to show us some new thing, or, as far as wood and windows can speak, to let us understand what would be the consequence of those antichristian figments that were brought into the church at first by him.

For can it be imagined but that, since so much confusion was brought into the church, some of the truly godly themselves would be much damnified thereby? The apostle says, "Evil communication corrupts good manners" (1 Cor 15:33). And that "their word will eat as doth a canker" (1 Tim 2:17). Mischief therefore must needs follow this ugly deed of the man of sin. If a house be on fire, though it is not burnt down, the smell of the flame may long remain there; also we count it no wonder to see some of the effects upon the rafters, beams, and some of the principal posts thereof. The calf that was set up at Dan defiled that people until the captivity of the land (Judg 18:30).

And I say again, since light against light was so early in the church in the wilderness, and has also been there so long, and again, since many in this church were both born and bred there under these oppositions of light, it is easy to conclude that something of the enemy's darkness might be also called light by the sincere that followed after. For by antichristian darkness, though they might call it light, the true light was darkened, and so the eye made dim, even the eye of the truly godly. Also the Holy Ghost did much withdraw itself from the church, so the doctrines, traditions, and rudiments of the world took more hold there, and spread themselves more formidably over the face of that whole church. For after the first angel had sounded, and the star was fallen from heaven to the earth, and had received the key of the bottomless pit, and had opened the mouth thereof, the smoke came out amain. This angel was one of the first dads of antichristianism, and this smoke was that which they call light, but it was "light against light." "And he opened the bottomless pit, and there arose a smoke out of the pit, as the smoke of a great furnace, and the sun and the air were darkened, by reason of the smoke of the pit" (Rev 9:1,2).

The sun I take to be the gospel of God, and the air a type of the breathings of the Holy Ghost. The smoke I take to be the doctrines and traditions of Antichrist; that which was, as I said before, put for light against the true light of the Word. Now, since the sun and the air were darkened by this smoke, yea, and so darkened as that the sun, nor moon, nor stars, nor day, nor night, could shine for a third part of them; no marvel though the true worshippers here were benighted, or, at least, had but little light to walk by; yea, I have known some that have been born and bred up in smokey holes, that have been made, both in smell and sight, to carry the tokens of their so being bred about them.

And I say again, as to what is now under our consideration, no marvel if they that breathed in this church in the wilderness, after the smoke came out of this pit, sucked in the smoke with the air until it became natural to them. A house annoyed with smoke is a great offence to the eyes, whose light being thereby impaired, the judgment also, since that, as to visibles, is guided by the eye, must needs be in danger of being in part misled. And this being the effect of light against light at first, is the cause of what to this day we see in the church among the true brotherhood. For as a cause produceth an effect, so oftentimes an effect sets on foot another cause.

Now, therefore, we have light against light among the godly, as afore there was antichristian against the Christian light. Not that light against light is now godly in the all of it. It is antichristian that opposes the Christian light still. But, as before, the darkness that opposed the light was in the antichristians, now that darkness is got into the Christians, and has set them against one another. Light therefore against light now is in the Christians, truly prefigured by that which was in the house of the forest of Lebanon. Witness the jars, the oppositions, the contentions, emulations, strifes, debates, whisperings, tumults, and condemnations that, like cannon-shot, have so frequently on all sides been let fly against one another.

Shall I need to mention particularly contests many years past, and presented to us in print? Words and papers now in print, as also the many petty divisions and names amongst us, sufficiently make this manifest. Wherefore light against light in this last place, or where it is thus repeated, cannot, I think, be more fitly applied than to that now under our consideration; that is to say, than to the opposite persuasions, different apprehensions, and thwart conclusions, that are constantly drawn from the same texts to maintain a diverse practice. Though we are to acknowledge with thankfulness that this opposition lies not so much in fundamentals as in things of a lesser import.

The godly all hold the head, for there Antichrist could never divide them; their divisions therefore are, as I said, only about smaller things. I do not say that the antichristian darkness has done nothing in the church as to the hurting it in the great things of God. But, I say, it has not been able to do that which could sever their Head from them, otherwise there appears even too much of the effect of his doings there. For even, as to the offices of our Lord, some will have his authority more large, some more strait. Some confine his rules to themselves and to their more outward qualification, and some believe they are extended further. Some will have his power in his church purely spiritual, others again would have it mixed. Some count his Word perfect and sufficient to guide in all religious matters, others again hold that an addition of something human is necessary. Some are for confining of his benefits, in the saving effects of them, only to the elect, others are for a stretching of them further. I might here multiply things, but that light against light is now among the godly as light against light was in the house of the forest of Lebanon, is not at all to be questioned.

This therefore may stand for another argument to prove that the house of the forest of Lebanon was a type of the church in the wilderness. As to the number here, that is to say, in three ranks, it is also, as I think, to show that, though, as was said afore, this darkness could not sever the true church from her Head, yet it has eclipsed the glory of things. By two lights a man cannot see this or that thing so exactly as by one single light; no, they both make all confused though they make not all invisible (Matt 6:22,23).

As, for instance, sun-light and moon-light together, fire- light and sun-light together, candle-light and moon-light together, make things more obscure than to look on them by a single light. The Word reflecting upon the understanding, without the interposing of man's traditions, makes the mind of God to a man more clear than when attended with the other. How much more then when light shall be against light in three ranks? Christ in his offices, blessed be God, is to this day known in his church, notwithstanding there is yet with us light against light in three ranks. But in these things he is not so distinctly, fully, and completely known, as he was before the church went into the wilderness. No, that knowledge is lost to a "third part" of it, as was also showed before (Rev 8:12).

Things therefore will never be well in the church of God so long as there is thus light against light therein. When there is but one Lord among us and his name One, and when divisions, by the consent of the whole, are banished, I mean, not persecuted, but abandoned in all by a joint consent, and when every man shall submit his own single opinion to those truths, that by their being retained are for the health of all, then look for good days, and not until then. For this house of the forest of Lebanon, in which, as you see, there is "light against light in three ranks," was not built to prefigure the church in her primitive state, but to show us how we should be while standing before the face of the dragon, and while shifting for ourselves in the wilderness.

And although by her pillars, and beauty, and tower, aye, and by her facing the very metropolitan of her enemies, she showeth that the true grace of God is in her, and a strength and courage that is invincible, yet for that she has also affixed to her station "Light against light in three ranks." It is evident her eye is not so single, and consequently that her body is not so full of light, as she will be when her sackcloth is put off, and as when she has put on her beautiful garments. For then it is that her moon is to shine as the sun, and that the light of her sun is to be sevenfold, even as the light of seven days, then, I say, "When the Lord bindeth up the breach of his people, and healeth the stroke of their wound" (Isa 30:26).

You know that a kingdom flourishes not so long as it is the seat of war, but when that is over peace and prosperity flourishes. This house, as has been hinted, was a type of the church in a wood, a forest, a wilderness.

CHAPTER VIII: OF THE SHIELDS AND TARGETS THAT WERE IN THE HOUSE OF THE FOREST OF LEBANON

As this house of the forest of Lebanon was that which, in the general, prefigured the state of the church in the wilderness, so it was accoutered with such military materials as suited her in such a condition, that is to say, with shields, and targets; consequently with other warlike things. "And king Solomon made two hundred targets of beaten gold, six hundred shekels of gold went to one target, and he made three hundred shields of beaten gold; [three pound] or three hundred shekels of gold went to one shield. And the king put them in the house of the forest of Lebanon" (1 Kings 10:16,17; 2 Chron 9:15,16).

This supposes that the house of the forest of Lebanon would be attacked by the enemy. And good reason there was for such a supposition, since it was built for defence of that worship that was set up in the church. Hence it is said, when the enemy used to come with his chariots and horsemen against them, that they "did look in that day to the armour of the house of the forest" (Isa 22:7,8). That was, to see how they were prepared at Lebanon, to make resistance against their foes, and to secure themselves and their religion from that destruction that by the enemy was designed should be made upon both. And thus again, or in this thing, the house of the forest of Lebanon shows that it was a figure of the church of the wilderness; for she also is furnished with such weapons as were counted by the wisdom of God necessary for the security of the soul, and Christian religion, to wit, "the weapons of our warfare," "the whole armour of God" (2 Cor 10:4).

For though this house of the forest of Lebanon was a place of defence, yet her armour is described and directed too, both as to matter and to measure. It was armour made of gold, such armour, and so much of it. And it was made by direction of Solomon, who was a type of Christ, by the power of whose grace and working our armour is also provided for us, as in the texts afore-mentioned may appear. By this description, therefore, of the armour of the house of the forest of Lebanon we are confined, that being a type to the armour of God, in the antitype thereto for the defence of the Christian religion. We then may make use of none but the armour of God for defence of our souls, and the worship of God; this alone is the golden armour provided by our Solomon, and put in the house of the forest of Lebanon, or rather in the church in the wilderness, for her to resist the enemy withal.

Two hundred targets. There is but little mention made of targets in the Bible, nor at all expressly how they were used, but once; and that was when Goliah came to defy Israel, he came, as with other warlike furniture, so "with a target of brass between his shoulders" (1 Sam 17:6). A target, that is, saith the margin, a gorget. A gorget is a thing wore about the neck, and it serveth in that place instead of a shield. Wherefore in some of your old Bibles, that which in one place is called a target, in another is called a shield. A shield for that part. This piece of armour, I suppose, was worn in old time by them that used spears, and it was to guard the upper part of the back and shoulders from the arrows of their enemies, that were shot into the air, to the intent they might fall upon the upper part of the body.

The shields were for them which drew bows, and they were to catch or beat off those arrows that were levelled at them by the enemy before. "Asa had" at one time "an army of men that bare targets and spears, out of Judah three hundred thousand, and out of Benjamin that bare shields, and drew bows, two hundred and fourscore thousand" (2 Chron 14:8).

I cannot tell what the target should signify here, unless it was to show that those in the type were more weak and faint-hearted than those in the antitype: for in that this gorget was prepared for some back part of the body, it supposed the wearers subject to run away, to flee. But in the description of the Christian armour, we have no provision for the back; so our men in the church in the wilderness are supposed to be more stout. Their face is made strong against the face of their enemies, and their foreheads strong against their foreheads (Eze 3:8,9). The shield was a type of the Christian faith, and so the apostle applies it. The which he also counteth a principal piece of our Christian armour when he saith, "Above all taking the shield of faith, wherewith ye shall be able to quench all the fiery darts of the wicked" (Eph 6:16). These targets and shields were made of gold, to show the excellent worth of this armour of God; to wit, that it is not carnal but spiritual, not human but divine; nor common or mean, but of an infinite value. Wherefore James, alluding to this, saith, "Hearken, my beloved brethren, Hath not God chosen the poor of this world rich in faith," (hath he not given them this golden shield) and made them "heirs of the kingdom which he hath promised to them that love him?" (James 2:5).

Faith! Peter saith, faith, in the very trial of it, is much more precious than is gold that perisheth. If so, then what is that worth, or value, that is in the grace itself? (1 Peter 1:7). This also is that which Christ intends when he says, "buy of me gold tried in the fire, that thou mayest be rich" (Rev 3:18).

And methinks the apostles and the Lord Jesus Christ do in all these places allude to the shields, the shields of gold, that Solomon made, and put in the house of the forest of Lebanon; which house, as I have showed, was that which indeed prefigured the state of the church in the wilderness; and these shields a type of faith.

Obj. But here is mention made of nothing but shields and targets.

Answ. True, and that perhaps to show us that the war that the church makes with Antichrist is rather defensive than offensive. Shields and targets are weapons defensive, weapons provided for self-preservation, not to hurt others with. A Christian also, if he can but defend his soul in the sincere profession of the true religion, doth what by duty, as to this, he is bound. Wherefore though the New Testament admits him to put on the whole armour of God, yet the whole and every part thereof is spiritual, and only defensive. True, there is mention made of the sword, but that sword "is the Word of God" (Eph 6:17). A weapon that hurteth none, none at all but the devil and sin, and those that love it. Indeed it was made for Christians to defend themselves, and their religion with, against hell and the angels of darkness. These two pieces of armour then that Solomon the king did put into the house of the forest of Lebanon, were types of the spiritual armour that the church in the wilderness should make use of. And as we read of no more that was put there, at least to be typical, so we read of, and must use no more than we are bid to put on by the apostle, for the defence of true religion.

Obj. But he that shall use none other than this, must look to come off a loser.

Answ. In the judgment of the world this is true; but not in the judgment of them that have skill, and a heart to use it. For this armour is not Saul's, which David refused, but God's, by which the lives of all those have been secured that put it on, and handled it well. You read of some of David's mighty men of valour, that their "faces were like the faces of lions, and" that they "were as swift" of foot "as the roes upon the mountains" (1 Chron 12:8). Being expert in handling spear and shield.

Why, God's armour makes a man's face look thus, also it makes him that useth it more lively and active than before. God's armour is no burden to the body, nor clog to the mind, but rather a natural, instead of an artificial, fortification.

But this armour comes not to any but out of the king's hand; Solomon put these targets and shields into the house of the forest of Lebanon. So Christ distributeth his armour to his church. Hence it is said it is given to his to suffer for him. It is given to his by himself, and on his behalf (Phil 1:29).

That is, that they might with it fight those battles which he shall manage against Antichrist. Hence they are called the armies in heaven, and are said to follow their Lord "upon white horses clothed in fine linen, white and clean." But, as I said, still their war was but defensive. For a little further do but observe, and you shall find the beast fall upon him. "And I saw the beast, and the kings of the earth, and their armies gathered together, to make war against him that sat on the horse, and against his army" (Rev 19:14,19). It is they that fall on, it is they that pick the quarrel, and give the onset. Besides, the armour, as I said, is only spiritual; wherefore the slaughter must needs be spiritual also. Hence as here it is said the Lamb did slay his enemies, by the sword, spirit, or breath of his mouth; so his army also slays them by the fire that proceedeth out of his mouth (Rev 1:16, 19:21).

Here is therefore no man's person in danger by this war. And I say again, so far as any man's person is in danger, it is by wrong managing of this war. True, the persons of the Christians are in danger, but that is because of the bloody disposition of an antichristian enemy. But we speak now with reference to the Lamb and the army that follows him; and as to them, no man's person is in danger simply as such. Wherefore, it is not men but sin; not men, but the man of sin, that wicked one, that the Son of God makes war against, in and by his church (2 Thess 2:8; Heb 12:4).

Let us therefore state the matter right; no man needs be afraid to let Jesus Christ be chief in the world, he envies nobody, he designs the hurt of none: his kingdom is not of this world, nor doth he covet temporal matters; let but his wife, his church alone, to enjoy her purchased privileges, and all shall be well. Which privileges of hers, since they are soul concerns, make no infringement upon any man's liberties. Let but faith and holiness walk the streets without control, and you may be as happy as the world can make you. I speak now to them that contend with him.

But if seasonable counsel will not go down, if hardness of heart and blindness of mind, and so perishing from the way, shall overtake you, it is but what you of old have been cautioned of. "Be wise now therefore, O ye kings; be instructed, ye judges of the earth. Serve the Lord with fear, and rejoice with trembling. Kiss the Son, lest he be angry, and ye perish from the way, when his wrath is kindled but a little. Blessed are all they that put their trust in him" (Psa 2:10-12).

Now let this also that has been said upon this head, be another argument to prove that the house of the forest of Lebanon was a type of the church in the wilderness.

CHAPTER IX: OF THE VESSELS WHICH SOLOMON PUT IN THE HOUSE OF THE FOREST OF LEBANON

Solomon did also put vessels into the house of the forest of Lebanon. "And all king Solomon's drinking-vessels were of gold, and all the vessels of the house of the forest of Lebanon were of" gold, "pure gold, none were of silver; it was nothing accounted of in the days of Solomon" (1 Kings 10:21; 2 Chron 9:20).

Since it is not expressed what those vessels of pure gold were which Solomon put in the house of the forest of Lebanon, therefore, as to the affirmative, no man can be absolute; vessels of gold, vessels of pure gold, the Holy Ghost says they were, and so leaves it to the prudent to make their conjectures; and although I may not put myself among the number of those prudent ones, yet let me take leave to say what I think in the case.

First then, negatively, they were not vessels ordained for Divine worship, for as that was confined to the temple, so the vessels and materials and circumstances for worship were there. I say, the whole uniform worship of the Jews now was confined to the temple (1 Chron 2:4, 7:12,15,16). Wherefore the vessels here mentioned could not be such as was in order to set up worship here, for to Jerusalem they were to bring their sacrifices; true, they had synagogues where ordinary service was done, there the law was read, and there the priests taught the people how they should serve the Lord; but for that which stood in carnal ordinances, as sacrificings, washings, and using vessels for that purpose, that was performed at Jerusalem.

This house, therefore, to wit, the house of the forest of Lebanon, was not built to slay or to offer burnt-offerings or sacrifices in, but as that altar was which the two tribes and an half, built by Jordan, when they went each to their inheritance, namely, to be a witness of the people's resolutions to preserve true religion in the church, to themselves, and to their posterity (Josh 22:21-29). Since this house therefore was designed for defensive war, it was not requisite that the formalities of worship should be there.

The church in the wilderness also, so far as she is concerned in contention, so far she is not taken up in the practical parts of religion (1 Thess 2:2); for religion is not to be practised in the church in the moments of contention. Let us practise then our religion in peace, and in all peaceable ways, and vindicate it by way of contention, that is, when asked or required by opposites to render a reason thereof (Phil 1:7,17; Acts 22:1). But my contention must be, not in pragmatic languages or in striving about words to no profit, but by words of truth and soberness, with all meekness and fear (Acts 26:24,25; Titus 3:1,2; 1 Peter 3:15).

To practise and defend a practice you know are two things; I practise religion in my closet, in my family, in the congregation, but I defend this practice before the magistrate, the king, and the judge. Now the temple was prepared for the practice of religion, and the house of the forest of Lebanon for defence of the same (Rev 11:1). So far then as the church in the wilderness worships, so far she is compared to the temple, and so far as she defends that worship, so far she is called an army (Rev 19:14). An army terrible with banners (Cant 6:4). For God has given a banner to them that fear him, that it may be displayed because of the truth (Psa 60:4). Hence she says to God, "We will rejoice in thy salvation, and in the name of our God, we will set up our banners" (Psa 20:5). But here is in all this no hurt to the world, the kingdom, the worship, the war is spiritual, even as the armour is. I have spoken this to distinguish worship from contending for worship, and to make way for what is yet to be said.

If the vessels of the forest of Lebanon, or those put in that house, were not such as related to worship, to worship simply as such, then it should seem—

These vessels therefore were for some other use than for formal worship in the house of the forest of Lebanon. The best way then, that I know of, to find out what they were is first to consider to what they are joined in the mention of them. Now I find them joined in the mention of them with Solomon's drinking vessels, and since as they were made of fine or pure gold, I take them also to be vessels of the same kind, namely, vessels to drink in. Now if we join to this the state of the church in the wilderness, of which, as we have said, this house of the forest of Lebanon was a type, then we must understand that by these vessels were prefigured such draughts as the church has, when in a bewildered or persecuted state; and they are of two sorts, either, First, Such as are exceeding bitter; or, Second, Such as are exceeding sweet; for both these attend a state of war.

First. Such as are exceeding bitter. These are called cups of red wine, signifying blood; also, the cup of the Lord's fury, the cup of trembling, the cup of astonishment, &c. (Psa 75:8; Isa 51:17,22; Jer 25:15; Eze 23:33).

Nor is there anything more natural to the church, while in a wilderness condition, than such cups and draughts as these. Hence she, as there, is said to be clothed, as was said afore, in sackcloth, to mourn, to weep, to cry out, and to be in pain, as is a woman in travail. See the Lamentations and you will find all this verified. See also Revelation 11:3, 12:2.

And whoso considers what has already been said as to what the house of the forest of Lebanon met with, will find that what is here inferred is not foreign but natural. For, can it be imagined, that when the king of Assyria laid down his army by the sides of Lebanon, and when the fire was to devour her cedars, also when Lebanon was to be cut down and languish, that these vessels, these cups, were not then put into her hand. And I say again, since the church in the wilderness, Lebanon's antitype, has been so persecuted, so distressed, so oppressed, and made the seat of so much war, so much blood, of so many murders of her children within her, &c., can it be imagined that she drank of none of these cups? Yes, yes, she has drank the red wine at the Lord's hand, even the cup of blood, of fury, of trembling, and of astonishment; witness her own cries, sighs, tears, and tremblings, with the cries of widows, children, and orphans within her (Lam 1, 2, 4, 5).

But what do I cite particular texts, since reason, histories, experience, anything that is intelligible, will confirm this for a truth; namely, that a people whose profession is directly in opposition to the devil and Antichrist, and to all debauchery, inhumanity, profaneness, superstition, and idolatry, when suffered to be invaded by the dragon, the beast, the false prophet, and whore, must needs taste of these cups, and drink thereof, to their astonishment.

But all these are of pure gold. They are of God's ordaining, appointing, filling, timing, and also sanctified by him for good to those of his that drink them. Hence Moses chose rather to drink a brimmer of these, "than to enjoy the pleasures of sin for a season" (Heb 11:25). The sourness, bitterness, and wormwood of them, therefore, is only to the flesh that loveth neither God, nor Christ, nor grace (Psa 75:8; Phil 1:28).

The afflictions, therefore, that the church in the wilderness hath met with, these cups of gold, are of more worth than are all the treasures of Egypt; they are needful and profitable, and praiseworthy also, and tend to the augmenting of our glory when the next world is come (1 Thess 3:3; Rev 2:10; 1 Peter 1:6). Besides they are signs, tokens, and golden marks of love, and jewels that set off the beauty of the church in the sight of God the more (Gal 6:17; Rev 3:19; Heb 12:6). They are also a means by which men are proved sound, honest, faithful, and true lovers of God, as also such whose graces are not counterfeit, feigned, or unsound, but true, and such as will be found to praise, and honour, and glory, at the appearing of Jesus Christ (Isa 27:9; Heb 12:7-10; 1 Peter 2:19; 2 Cor 4:17,18; 2 Thess 1:5).

And this has been the cause that the men of our church in the wilderness have gloried in tribulation, taking pleasure in reproaches, in necessities, in persecutions, and in distresses for Christ's sake (Rom 5:3; 2 Cor 12:9,10). Yea, this is the reason why they have bidden one another rejoice when they fell into divers temptations, saying, Happy is the man that endureth temptations, and behold we count them happy that endure (James 1:2,12, 5:11). And again, "if ye be reproached for the name of Christ, happy are ye" (1 Peter 4:14).

These therefore are vessels of pure gold, though they contain such bitter draughts, and though such as at which we make so many wry faces before we can get their liquor down.

Do you think that a Christian, having even this cup in his hand to drink it, would change it for a draught of that which is in the hand of the woman that sits on the back of the scarlet-coloured beast? (Rev 17:3,4). No, verily, for he knows that her sweet is poison, and that his bitter is to purge his soul, body, life, and religion, of death (2 Tim 2:11,12).

God sends his love tokens to his church two ways, sometimes by her friends, sometimes by her enemies. When they come by the hand of a friend, as by a minister, a brother, or by the Holy Ghost, then they come smoothly, sweetly, and are taken, and go down like honey. But when these love tokens come to them by the hand of an enemy, then they are handed to them roughly; Pharaoh handed love tokens to them roughly; the king of Babylon handed these love tokens to them roughly. They bring them of malice, God sends them of love; they bring them and give them to us, hoping they will be our death; they give us them therefore with many a foul curse, but God blesses them still. Did not Haman lead Mordecai in his state by the hand of anger?

Nor is this cup so bitter but that our Lord himself drank deep of it before it was handed to his church; he did as loving mothers do, drink thereof himself to show us it is not poison, also to encourage us to drink it for his sake and for our endless health (Matt 20:22, 26:39,42).

And, as I told you before, I think I do not vary from the sense of the text in calling them cups; because, though there they have no name, they are joined with king Solomon's drinking vessels, and because as so joined in the type, so they are also joined here; therefore the cup here is called Christ's cup. "Are ye able to drink of the cup that I shall drink of?" "Ye shall drink indeed of my cup" (Matt 20:22,23). Here you see they are joined in a communion in this cup of affliction, as the cups in one and the same breath are joined with those king Solomon drank in, which he put in the house of the forest of Lebanon.

[Second. Such as are exceeding sweet.]

But these are not all the cups that belong to the house of the forest of Lebanon, or rather to the church in the wilderness; there is also a cup, out of which, at times, is drunk what is exceeding sweet. It is called the cup of consolation, the cup of salvation; a cup in the which God himself is (Psa 116:13; Jer 16:7). As he said, the Lord is the portion of my cup. Or rather, "The Lord is the portion of mine inheritance, and my cup" (Psa 16:5). This cup, they that are in the church in the wilderness have usually for an after-draught to that bitter one that went before. Thus, as tender mothers give their children plumbs or sugar, to sweeten their palate after they have drank a bitter potion, so God gives his the cups of salvation and consolation, after they have suffered awhile. "For as the sufferings of Christ abound in us, so our consolation also aboundeth by Christ" (2

Cor 1:5).

Hence the apostle assureth himself concerning the affliction of them at Corinth; yea, and also promiseth them, that as they were partakers of the sufferings, so should they be of the consolation (2 Cor 1:7). Some of these cups are filled until they run over, as David said his did, when the valley of the shadow of death was before him. "Thou preparest a table before me," said he, "in the presence of mine enemies: thou anointest my head with oil; my cup runneth over" (Psa 23:5). This is that which the apostle calls exceeding; that is, that which is beyond measure. "I am," says he, "filled with comfort, I am exceeding joyful in all our tribulation" (2 Cor 7:4).

Now he has one answering the other. Thou hast made summer and winter. Thou hast made the warm beams of thy sun answerable to the cold of the dark night. This may be also yet signified by the building of this house, this type of the church in the wilderness, in so pleasant a place as the forest of Lebanon was (Cant 4:8). Lebanon! Lebanon was one of the sweetest places in all the land of Canaan. Therefore we read of the fruit of Lebanon, of the streams from Lebanon; the scent, the smell, the glory of Lebanon; and also of the wine and flowers of Lebanon (Psa 72:16; Hosea 14:6,7; Isa 35:2, 9:13; Nahum 1:4).

Lebanon! That was one thing that wrought with Moses to desire that he might go over Jordan; namely, that he might see that goodly mountain, and Lebanon. The glory and excellent beauty of the church, Christ also setteth forth, by comparing of her to Lebanon. "Thy lips, O my spouse," says he, "drop as the honey-comb: honey and milk are under thy tongue, and the smell of thy garment is like the smell of Lebanon" (Cant 4:11,15). This house, therefore, being placed here, might be to show how blessed a state God could make the state of his church by his blessed grace and presence, even while she is in a wilderness condition.

We will add to this, for further demonstration, that letter of that godly man, Pomponius Algerius, an Italian martyr; some of the words of which are these:—

"Let," saith he, "the miserable worldly man answer me; what remedy or safe refuge can there be unto him if he lack God, who is the life and medicine of all men: and how can he be said to fly from death, when he himself is already dead in sin. If Christ be the way, verity, and life, how can there be any life then without Christ?

"The sooly heat of the prison to me is coldness; the cold winter to me is a fresh spring-time in the Lord. He that feareth not to be burned in the fire, how will he fear the heat of weather? Or what careth he for the pinching frost, which burneth with the love of the Lord?

"The place is sharp and tedious to them that be guilty; but to the innocent and guiltless it is mellifluous. Here droppeth the delectable dew; here floweth the pleasant nectar; here runneth the sweet milk; here is plenty of all good things. And although the place itself be desert and barren, yet to me it seemeth a large walk, and a valley of pleasure; here to me is the better and more noble part of the world. Let the miserable worldling say, and confess, if there be any plot, pasture, or meadow, so delightful to the mind of man, as here. Here I see kings, princes, cities, and people; here I see wars, where some be overthrown, some be victors, some thrust down, some lifted up. Here is Mount Sion; here I am already in heaven itself. Here standeth first Christ Jesus in the front; about him stand the old fathers, prophets, and evangelists, apostles, and all the servants of God; of whom some do embrace and cherish me, some exhort me, some open the sacraments unto me, some comfort me, other some are singing about me: and how then shall I be thought to be alone, among so many, and such as these be, the beholding of whom to me is both solace and example. For here I see some crucified, some slain, some stoned, some cut asunder, and some quartered, some roasted, some broiled, some put in hot caldrons, some having their eyes bored through, some their tongues cut out, some their skin plucked over their heads, some their hands and feet chopped off, some put in kilns and furnaces, some cast down headlong, and given to the beasts and fowls of the air to feed upon. It would," said he, "ask a long time, if I should recite all.

"To be short, divers I see with divers and sundry torments excruciate; yet notwithstanding, all living and all safe. One plaster, one salve cureth all their wounds, which also giveth to me strength and life; so that I sustain all these transitory anguishes and small afflictions with a quiet mind, having a greater hope laid up in heaven. Neither do I fear mine adversaries which here persecute me and oppress me, for he that dwelleth in heaven shall laugh them to scorn, and the Lord shall deride them. I fear not thousands of people which compass me about. The Lord my God shall deliver me, my hope, my supporter, my comforter, who exalteth up my head. He shall smite all them that stand up against me without cause; and shall dash the teeth and jaws of sinners asunder, for he only is all blessedness and majesty.

"The rebukes for Christ's cause make us jocund; for so it is written: if ye be rebuked and scorned for the name of Christ, happy be you; for the glory and spirit of God resteth upon you (1 Peter 4). Be ye therefore certified (said he, by this his letter to his friends) that our rebukes, which are laid upon us, redound to the shame and harm of the rebukers. In this world there is no mansion firm to me; and therefore I will travel up to the New Jerusalem which is in heaven, and which offereth itself to me, without paying any fine or income. Behold I have entered already in my journey, where my house standeth for me prepared, and where I shall have riches, kinsfolks, delights, honours, never- failing.

"As for these earthly things here present, they are transitory shadows, vanishing vapours, and ruinous walls. Briefly all is but very vanity of vanities, whereas hope, and the substance of eternity to come, are wanting; which the merciful goodness of the Lord hath given, as companions to accompany me, and to comfort me; and now do the same begin to work, and to bring forth fruits in me. I have travelled hitherto, laboured and sweat early and late, watching day and night, and now my travails begin to come to effect. Days and hours have I bestowed upon my studies. Behold the true countenance of God is sealed upon me, the Lord hath given mirth in my heart: and therefore in the same will I lay me down in peace and rest (Psa 4). And who then shall dare to blame this our age consumed; or say that our years be cut off? What man can now cavil that these our labours are lost, which have followed, and found out the Lord and maker of the world, and which have changed death with life? My portion is the Lord, saith my soul, and therefore, I will seek and wait for him.

"Now then, if to die in the Lord be not to die but live most joyfully, where is this wretched worldly rebel, which blameth us of folly, for giving away our lives to death? O how delectable is this death to me! to taste the Lord's cup, which is an assured pledge of true salvation; for so hath the Lord himself forewarned us, saying, the same that they have done to me, they will also do unto you. Wherefore let the doltish world, with his blind worldlings (who in the bright sunshine, yet go stumbling in darkness, being as blind as beetles), cease thus unwisely to carp against us for our rash suffering, as they count it. To whom, thus, we answer again, with the holy apostle, that neither tribulation, nor anguish, nor hunger, nor nakedness, nor jeopardy, nor persecution, nor sword, shall be able ever to separate us from the love of Christ; we are slain all the day long; we are made like sheep ordained to the shambles (Rom 8).

"Thus," saith he, "do we resemble Christ our Head, which said that the disciple cannot be above his master, nor the servant about his Lord. The same Lord hath also commanded that every one shall take up his cross and follow him (Luke 9). Rejoice, rejoice, my dear brethren and fellow-servants, and be of good comfort, when ye fail into sundry temptations; let your patience be perfect in all parts. For so it is foreshowed us before, and is written, that they which shall kill you shall think to do God good service. Therefore, afflictions and death be as tokens and sacraments of our election and life to come. Let us then be glad and sing unto the Lord, when as we, being clear from all just accusations, are persecuted and given to death; for better it is that we in doing well do suffer, if it so be the will of God, than doing evil (1 Peter 3). We have for our example Christ and the prophets which spake in the name of the Lord, whom the children of iniquity did quell and murder. And now we bless and magnify them that then suffered. Let us be glad and joyous in our innocency and uprightness; the Lord shall reward them that persecute us; let us refer all revengement to him.

"I am accused of foolishness, for that I do not shrink from the true doctrine and knowledge of God, and do not rid myself out of these troubles, when with one word I may. O the blindness of man, which seeth not the sun shining, neither remembereth the Lord's words. Consider therefore what he saith, you are the light of the world. A city built on the hill cannot be hid; neither do men light a candle and put it under a bushel, but upon a candlestick, that it may shine, and give light to them in the house. And in another place he saith you shall be led before kings and rulers. Fear ye not them which kill the body, but him which killeth both body and soul. Whosoever shall confess me before men, him will I also confess before my Father which is in heaven; and he that denieth me before men, him will I also deny before my heavenly Father.

"Wherefore, seeing the words of the Lord be so plain, how, or by what authority, will this wise counsellor then approve this his counsel which he doth give? God forbid that I should relinquish the commandments of God and follow the counsels of men. For it is written, Blessed is the man that hath not gone in the way of sinners, and hath not stood in the counsels of the ungodly, and hath not sit in the chair of pestilence (Psa 1). God forbid that I should deny Christ where I ought to confess him; I will not set more by my life than by my soul, neither will I exchange the life to come for this world here present. O how foolishly speaketh he which argueth me of foolishness!"

And a little farther he saith, "And now let this carnal politic counsellor, and disputer of this world, tell wherein have they to blame me. If in mine examinations I have not answered so after their mind and affection as they required of me, seeing it is not ourselves that speak, but the Lord that speaketh in us, as he himself doth fore-witness, saying, When you shall be brought before rulers and magistrates, it is not you yourselves that speak, but the Spirit of my Father that shall be in you (Matt 10). Wherefore, if the Lord be true and faithful of his word, as it is most certain, then there is no blame in me; for he gave the words that I did speak, and who was I that could resist his will?

"If any man shall reprehend the things that I said, let him then quarrel with the Lord, whom it pleased to work so in me; and if the Lord be not to be blamed, neither am I herein to be accused, which did that I purposed not, and that I fore-thought not of. The things that there I did utter and express [he means when he was before the magistrates], if they were otherwise than well, let them show it, and then will I say that they were my words, and not the Lord's. But if they were good and approved, and such as cannot justly be accused, then must it needs be granted, spite of their teeth, that they proceeded of the Lord; and then who be they that shall accuse me—people of prudence? Or who shall condemn me—just judges? And though they so do, yet, nevertheless, the word shall not be frustrate, neither shall the gospel be foolish or therefore decay, but rather the kingdom of God shall the more prosper and flourish unto the Israelites, and shall pass the sooner unto the elect of Christ Jesus, and they which shall so do shall prove the grievous judgment of God. Neither shall they escape without punishment that be persecutors and murderers of the just.

"My well-beloved," saith he, "lift up your eyes and consider the counsels of God. He showed unto us a late an image of his plague, which was to our correction; and if we shall not receive him he will draw out his sword and strike with sword, pestilence, and famine, the nation that shall rise against Christ."

This, as I said, is part of a letter writ by Pomponius Alerius, an Italian martyr, who, when he wrote it, was in prison, in, as he calls it, his delectable orchard, the prison of Leonine, 12 calend. August, anno 1555. As is to be seen in the second volume of the book of martyrs.

This man was, when he wrote this letter, in the house of the forest of Lebanon, in the church in the wilderness, in the place and way of contending for the truth of God, and he drank of both these bitter cups of which I spake before, to wit, of that which was exceeding bitter, and of that which was exceeding sweet, and the reason why he complained not of the bitter was because the sweet had overcome it—as his afflictions abounded for Christ, so did his consolations by him. So, did I say? they abounded much more.

But was not this man, think you, a giant, a pillar in this house? Had he not also now hold of the shield of faith? Yea, was he not now in the combat? And did he not behave himself valiantly? Was not his mind elevated a thousand degrees beyond sense, carnal reasons, fleshly love, self-concerns, and the desires of embracing temporal things? This man had got that by the end that pleased him; neither could all the flatteries, promises, threats, or reproaches, make him one listen to or desire to inquire after what the world or the glory of it could afford. His mind was captivated with delights invisible; he coveted to show his love to his Lord by laying down his life for his sake; he longed to be there where there shall be no more pain, nor sorrow, nor sighing, nor tears, nor troubles; he was a man of a thousand (Eccl 7:28).

But to return again to our text. You know we are now upon the vessels of the house of the forest of Lebanon, which, I have told you, could not be vessels for worship, for that worship that was ordained to be performed at the temple was also confined to that, and to the vessels that were there. Therefore they must be, in all probability, the vessels that I have mentioned, the which you see how we have expounded and applied. If I am out I know it not; if others can give me better light here about for it I will be thankful.

There was also added to this house of the forest of Lebanon, store-cities, chariot-cities, and cities of horsemen, unto which king Jotham added castles and towers (2 Chron 8:4-6, 27:3,4).

These might be to signify by what ways and means God would at times revenge the quarrel of his church, even in this world, upon them that, without cause, should, for their faith and worship, set themselves against them. For here is a face of threatening revenge, they were store-houses, chariot-cities, cities of horsemen, with castles and towers. And they stood on the same ground that this house was builded upon, even in the forest of Lebanon. We know that in Israel God stirred up kings who at times suppressed idolatry there, and plagued the persecutors too, as Jehu, Hezekiah, Josiah, &c. And he has promised that, even in gospel times, kings "shall hate the whore, - make her desolate and naked, and shall eat her flesh and burn her with fire" (Rev 17:12,16).

Here now are the store-houses, chariot-cities, cities of horsemen, with towers and castles, for the help to the house of the forest of Lebanon, for the help of the church in the wilderness, or, as you have it in another place, as the serpent cast floods of water out of his mouth after the woman, "that he might cause her to be carried away of the flood. And the earth helped the woman, and the earth opened her mouth and swallowed up the flood which the dragon cast out of his mouth" (Rev 12:15,16). Thus the Medes and Persians helped to deliver the church from the clutches and strong hand of the king of Babylon.

This Lebanon, therefore, was a place considerable and a figure of great things; the countenance of the Lord Jesus is compared to it, and so is the face of his spouse, and also the smell of her garment (Cant 4:11, 5:15, 7:4).

CHAPTER X: OF THE PORCH OF THE HOUSE OF THE FOREST OF LEBANON

Solomon also made a porch to this house of the forest of Lebanon. He made several porches, as one for the temple, one for the house which he dwelt in, one for the throne of the kingdom, and this that was for the house of the forest of Lebanon, of all which this last is that mentioned.

"And he made a porch of pillars, the length thereof was fifty cubits, and the breadth thereof thirty cubits; and the porch was before them, and the other pillars, and the thick beam were before them" (1 Kings 7:6). This porch was famous both for length, and breadth, and strength, it was able to contain a thousand men. It was like that of the tower of David, otherwise called the stronghold, the castle of Zion, which is the city of David (2 Sam 5:7; 1 Chron 11:5; Micah 4:8).

This tower of David was built for an armoury, whereon there hanged a thousand bucklers, all shields of mighty men. It was fifty cubits long and thirty broad, a spacious place, a large receptable for any that liked to take shelter there. It was made of pillars, even as the house within was, or it stood upon pillars. The pillars, you know I told you before, were to show us what mighty men, or what men of mighty grace, God would have in his church in the wilderness furnished with. And it is worth your observing here also we have pillars, pillars. And he made the porch of pillars, that is, of pillars of cedar, as the rest of the pillars of the house were.

"And the porch was before them." That is, as I take it, an entering porch, less than the space within, so that the pillars, neither as to number nor bigness, could be seen without, until at least they that had a mind to see entered the mouth of the porch. And by this was fitly prefigured how unseen the strength of the church under persecution is of all that are without her. Alas! they think that she will be run down with a push, or, as they said, "What do these feeble Jews? Will they fortify themselves? Will they sacrifice? Will they make an end in a day? Will they revive the stones out of the heaps of the rubbish which are bunt?" Alas! "if a fox go up he shall even break down their stone wall" (Neh 4:2,3).

But do you think these men saw the strength of the Jews now? No, no, their pillars were within, and so were shadowed from their eyes. David himself could not tell what judgment to make of the way of the world against the people of God, until he went into the sanctuary of God (Psa 73:16,17).

How then can the world judge of the condition of the saints? Alas, had they known the church's strength, surely they would not, as they have, so furiously assaulted the same. But what have they got by all they have done, either against the head or body of the same? She yet has being in the world, and will have, shall have, though all the nations on earth should gather themselves together against it. Nor is it the cutting off of many that will make her cease to flourish. Alas, were she not sometimes pruned and trimmed her boughs would stand too thick. Those therefore that are taken away with God's pruning-hooks are removed, that the under branches may grow the better. But, I say, to extinguish her it is in vain for any to hope for that. She stands upon pillars, on rocks, on the munition of rocks; stand therefore she must, whether the world believes it or no.

"And the other pillars - were before them," or, as the margin has it, "according to them." The other pillars, that is, they more inward, those that were in the body of the house. Christ doth not, as the poor world doth, that is, set the best leg before; the pillars that were more inward in the house were as good as those in the front. It is true some are appointed to death to show to the world the strength of grace, not that he can help nobody to that strength but they. The most feeble of his flock, when Christ shall stand by and strengthen them, are able to do and bear what the strong have underwent. For so he saith.

And "the other pillars and the thick beams were" according to them; nay, "before them." Indeed, they that are left seem weak and feeble if compared to them that have already been tried with fire and sword and all the tortures of men. But that grace by which they were helped that have done such mighty acts already, can help those who seem more weak yet to go beyond them. God strengtheneth "the spoiled against the strong, so that the spoiled shall come against the fortress" (Amos 5:9). Or, as another scripture has it, "The lame take the prey" (Isa 33:23). So that you see here is all substance. All here are pillars and thick beams, both in the house and in the porch.

The conclusion therefore is:—The true members of the church in the wilderness are strong, mighty, being made able by the grace of God for their standing, and being also coupled and compacted together with the biggest bands or thickest beams that the Holy Ghost puts forth to bind and hold this church together. And there is reason for it. The church is God's tower or battery by which he beateth down Antichrist, or if you will have it in the words of the prophet, "Thou art my battle-axe and weapons of war; for with thee [saith God] will I break in pieces," &c. (Jer 51:19,20). Wherefore, since the church is set for defence of religion, and to be as a battery to beat down Antichrist, it is requisite that she should be made up of pillars of strong and staunch materials.

The largeness of the porch was commodious; it was the next shelter, or the place whereunto they of the house of the forest of Lebanon, when pursued, might resort or retreat with the less difficulty. Thus the church in the wilderness has her porch, her place, her bosom, whereunto her discouraged may continually resort, and take up and be refreshed. As Abiathar thrust in to David and his men in the wilderness, in the day when Saul had slain his father, and of his brethren, even "four-score and five persons that did wear a linen ephod" (1 Sam 22:17-23).

When the apostles were persecuted "they went to their own company," because the Lord was there (Acts 4:23). There we find the pillars, and have both solace and example. There, as Pomponius said of his person, stands Christ Jesus in the front as Captain of the Lord's host, and round about him the old fathers, prophets, apostles, and martyrs. This porch, therefore, I take to be a figure of those cordial and large affections which the church in the wilderness has to all, and for all them that love the truth, and that suffer and are afflicted for the sincere profession thereof.

This porch was bigger than that which belonged to the temple by much, to show that those that are made the objects of the enemies' rage most are usually most prepared with affection for them that are in the same condition. Fellow-feeling is a great matter. It is said of the poor afflicted people that were in Macedonia "in a great trial of affliction, the abundance of their joy and their deep poverty abounded unto the riches of their liberality; for to their power, - yea, and beyond their power," they showed their charity to the destroyed church of Jerusalem (2 Cor 8:1-4).

And a porch in a forest, or a bosom in a wilderness, is seasonable to them that in the wilderness are faint and weary. Nabal shut up his doors against David, and therefore he died like a beast. Poor David! thou wast bewildered, but this churl had no compassion for thee (1 Sam 25:5-13, 25- 39). Blest Obadiah, thou hadst a bosom, and bread, and hiding-places for the church, when rent and torn by the fury of Jezebel, and thou hast for it thy reward in heaven (1 Kings 18:3,4; Matt 10:42). Ebedmelech, because he had compassion on Jeremiah when he was in the dungeon, God did not only give him his life for a prey, but promised him the effects of putting his trust in the Lord (Jer 38:7-11, 39:15-18).

And he made a porch of pillars. The porch is but the entrance of the house, whither many go that yet step not into the house, but make their retreat from thence; but it is because they are non-residents, they only come to see; or else, if they pretended more, it was not from the heart. "They went out from us," said John, "but they were not of us; for if they had been of us they would, no doubt, have continued with us; but they went out that they might be made manifest that they were not all of us" (1 John 2:19).

And forasmuch as this porch was fifty cubits long, men may take many a step straight forward therein and be but in the porch yet. Even as we have seen men go, as one would think, till they are out of view in the porch of this church in the wilderness, but presently you have them without the door again.

True, this porch was made of pillars, and so to every one, at first entrance, it showed the power of the place; the church in the wilderness also is so built that men may see it is ordained for defence. Men also, at their first offer to step over the threshold there, with mouth profess that they will dwell as soldiers there. But words are but wind; when they see the storm a-coming they will take care to shift for themselves. This house, or church in the wilderness, must see to itself for all them.

As the house therefore is a figure of the church in the wilderness, so, so great a porch belonging to it may be also to show that numbers may there be entertained that, if need be, will quickly whip out again. Although therefore the porch was made of pillars, yet every one that walked there were not such. The pillars was to show them, not what they were, but what they should be that entered into this house.

The church also in the wilderness, even in her porch or first entrance into it, is full of pillars, apostles, prophets, and martyrs of Jesus. There also hang up the shields that the old warriors have used, and are plastered upon the walls the brave achievements which they have done. There are also such encouragements there for those that stand, that one would think none that came thither with pretence to serve there would, for very shame, attempt to go back again; and yet, not to their credit be it spoken, they will forsake the place without blushing, yea, and plead for this their so doing. But I have done with the explicatory part, and conclude that from these ten particulars thus handled in this book, the house of the forest of Lebanon was a type, or figure, of the church in the wilderness.

Nor do I know, if this be denied, how so fitly to apply some of these texts which speak to the church, to support her under her troubles, of the comforts that afterwards she shall enjoy, since they are presented to her under such metaphors as clearly denote she was once in a wilderness, for instance,

1. "Sing, O ye heavens; for the Lord hath done it [that is, redeemed his servant Jacob from his sins and from the hand of the enemy]: shout, ye lower parts of the earth [or church once trampled under feet]: break forth into singing, ye mountains, O forest, and every tree therein [here is comfort for the church under the name of a forest, that in which the house we have been speaking of was built]: for the Lord hath redeemed Jacob, and glorified himself in Israel" (Isa 44:23). To what, I say, can this text more fitly be applied, than to the church in the wilderness, put here under the name of a forest as well as under the title of heaven? Yea, methinks it is cried here to her, "O forest," on purpose to intimate to us that the house in the forest of Lebanon was the figure of the church in this condition.

2. Again, "Is it not yet a very little while, and Lebanon shall be turned into a fruitful field, and the fruitful field shall be esteemed as a forest? And in that day shall the deaf hear the words of the book, and the eyes of the blind shall see out of obscurity, and out of darkness. The meek also shall increase their joy in the Lord, and the poor among men shall rejoice in the holy One of Israel. For the terrible one is brought to nought, and the scorner is consumed, and all that watch for iniquity are cut off" (Isa 29:17-20). Lebanon was a forest, but now she must be a fruitful field. What means he here by Lebanon but the church under persecution, and the fruitful field? Mistress Babylon shall become as a forest, that is, as the church under distress. But when shall this be? Why, when the terrible one is brought low and the scorner is consumed, &c.

What can be more plain than this to prove that Lebanon, even the house in the forest of Lebanon, for that is here intended, was a figure of the church in the wilderness, or in a tempted and persecuted state. For to be turned into a fruitful field signifies the recovering of the afflicted church into a state most quiet and fruitful; fruitful fields are quiet because they are fenced, and so shall the church be in that day.

3. "The wilderness and the solitary place shall be glad for them; and the desert shall rejoice, and blossom as the rose" (Isa 35:1).

What are we to understand by these words if they be not a prophecy of the flourishing state of Christ's kingdom, who, in the days of her persecution, is compared to a wilderness, to a desert, and to solitary places. And she "shall be glad for them"; for what? for that she is rid of the dragons, wild beasts, satyrs, screech owls, great owl, and vulture, types of the beasts and unclean birds of Antichrist (Isa 34:13-15).

She shall be glad for them that they are taken away from her and placed far away, for then no lion shall be there nor any ravenous beast; yea, it is the habitation of dragons, where each lay, shall be grass, with reeds and rushes, as it is, Isaiah 35. And now "the lame man shall leap as a hart, and the tongue of the dumb sing; for in the wilderness shall waters break out, and streams in the desert." Read the whole chapter.

For that the desert and wilderness is thus mentioned, and that to express the state of the church in trouble by, it is clear that Lebanon is not excluded, nor the thing that is signified thereby, which, I say, is the church in her low estate, in her forest, or wilderness condition.

4. "I will plant in the wilderness the cedar, the shittah-tree, and the myrtle, and the oil-tree; I will set in the desert the fir-tree, and the pine, and the box-tree together" (Isa 41:19).

Can any think that trees are the things taken care of here? They are the men that Antichrist has murdered in his heat and rage against Christ, the which God will restore again to his church, when Antichrist is dead and buried in the sides of the pit's mouth. And that you may the better understand he meaneth so, he expresseth again the state of the church as like to a wilderness condition, and promiseth that in that very church, now so like a wilderness, to plant it again with Christians, flourishing with variety of gifts and graces, signified by the various nature and name of the trees spoken of here.

5. "Behold, I will do a new thing; now it shall spring forth; shall ye not know it? I will even make a way in the wilderness, and rivers in the desert. The beast of the field shall honour me, the dragons and the owls: because I give waters in the wilderness, and rivers in the desert, to give drink to my people, my chosen" (Isa 43:19,20). Here God alludes to the condition of the children of Israel in the wilderness of old, and implies they shall be in a wilderness again; and as then he gave them water, and delivered them from serpents, cockatrices, vipers, dragons, so he will do now, now to his people, his chosen.

6. "The Lord shall comfort Zion: he will comfort all her waste places; and he will make her wilderness like Eden, and her desert like the garden of the Lord; joy and gladness shall be found therein, thanksgiving, and the voice of melody" (Isa 51:3).

See here are Zion's waste places, Zion's wilderness, forest, or Lebanon. Next here is a promise that he will comfort her; and what doth this suppose but that she was in her wilderness state, uncomfortable at least as to her outward peace, her liberty, and gospel privileges and beauties? Then here is the comparison, by which he illustrates his promise as to what degree and pitch he will comfort her. "He will make her wilderness like Eden, and her desert like the garden of the Lord." The effects of all which will be she will have joy and gladness; she will be thankful, and be melodious in her voice, in her soul to the Lord. This, I say, will follow upon her deliverance from her desert, her wilderness, her desolate, and comfortless state: all which is more fully expressed by her repeated hallelujahs (Rev 19:1- 6). Which hallelujahs there are the effect of her deliverance from the rage of the beast and great whore, of whose greatness and ruin you read in the two foregoing chapters. Now, I say, since the church was to be in a wilderness condition under the gospel; and since we have this house of the forest of Lebanon so particularly set forth in the Scriptures; and also since this house, its furniture, its troubles, and state, do so paint out this church in this wilderness state, I take it to be for that very thing designed, that is to say, to prefigure this church in this her so solitary and wilderness state.

CONCLUSION

We will now therefore here make a brief conclusion of all.

First. This may inform us of the reason of the deplorable state of a professing people. It is allotted to them in this world to be so. The world, and men of the world, must have their tranquility here, and must be possest of all; this was foreshown in Esau, who had of his sons many that were dukes and kings before there was any king in Israel (Gen 36:31). God so disposing of things that all may give place when his Son shall come to reign in Mount Zion, and before his ancients gloriously, which coming of his will be at the resurrection, and end of this world, and then shall his saints reign with him; "when Christ, who is our life, shall appear, then shall ye also appear with him in glory" (Col 3:4).

Let not therefore kings, and princes, and potentates be afraid; the saints that are such indeed, know their places, and are of a peaceable deportment; "the earth God hath given to the children of men," and his kingdom to the sons of God (Psa 115:16; Matt 25:34; Luke 12:32).

I know there are extravagant opinions in the world about the kingdom of Christ, as if it consisted in temporal glory in part, and as if he would take it to him by carnal weapons, and so maintain it in its greatness and grandeur; but I confess myself an alien to these notions, and believe and profess the quite contrary, and look for the coming of Christ to judgment personally, and betwixt this and that, for his coming in Spirit, and in the power of his word to destroy Antichrist, to inform kings, and so give quietness to his church on earth; which shall assuredly be accomplished,[23] when the reign of the beast, the whore, the false prophet, and of the man of sin is out (2 Thess 2:8; Isa 49:23, 52:15, 60:3,10,11,16, 62:2; Rev 21:24).

Second. Let this teach men not to think that the church is cursed of God, because she is put in a wilderness state. Alas, that is but to train her up in a way of solitariness, to make her Canaan the more welcome to her. Rest is sweet to the labouring man. Yea, this condition is the first step to heaven; yea, it is a preparation to that kingdom. God's ways are not as man's. "I have chosen thee," saith he, "in the furnace of affliction." When Israel came out of Egypt, they were led of

God into the wilderness; but why? That he might have them to a land, that he had espied for them, that he might bring them to a city of habitation (Eze 20:6; Psa 107:1-7).

The world know not the way of the Lord, nor the judgment of our God. Do you think that saints that dwell in the world, and that have more of the mind of God than the world, would, could so rejoice in God, in the cross, in tribulations and distresses, were they not assured that through many tribulations is the very roadway to heaven (Acts 14:22).

Let this then encourage the saints to hope, and to rejoice in hope of the glory of God, notwithstanding present tribulations. This is our seed-time, our winter; afflictions are to try us of what mettle we are made; yea, and to shake off worm-eaten fruit, and such as are rotten at core. Troubles for Christ's sake are but like the prick of an awl in the tip of the ear, in order to hang a jewel there.

Let this also put the saints upon patience: when we know that a trial will have an end, we are by that knowledge encouraged to exercise patience. I have a bad master, but I have but a year to serve under him, and that makes me serve him with patience; I have but a mile to go in this dirty way, and then I shall have my path pleasant and green, and this makes me tread the dirty way with patience. I am now in my rags, but by that a quarter of a year is come and gone, two hundred a year comes into my hand, wherefore I will wait, and exercise patience. Thus might I multiply comparisons. Be patient then, my brethren; but how long? to the coming of the Lord. But when will that be? the coming of the Lord draws nigh.

"Be patient," my brethren, be long patient, even "unto the coming of the Lord. Behold, the husbandman waiteth for the precious fruit of the earth, and hath long patience for it, until he receive the early and latter rain. Be ye also patient; stablish your hearts: for the coming of the Lord draweth nigh" (James 5:7,8).

Made in the USA
Coppell, TX
27 September 2021